12 R/5.

913333
15.

THE DEFIANT ONES

THE DEFIANT ONES

DRAMATIC STUDIES
OF MODERN SOCIAL REFORMERS

BRIAN PEACHMENT

*Master in charge of Drama, South Hunsley School,
Melton, North Ferriby, Yorkshire*

THE RELIGIOUS EDUCATION PRESS LTD.
(*A member of the Pergamon Group*)
HEADINGTON HILL HALL   OXFORD

£0.75

08   006441   8

© 1969 Brian Peachment

First published 1969
Library of Congress Catalog Card No. 69–19972

Printed in Great Britain by A. Wheaton & Co., Exeter

08 006441 8

CONTENTS

I suggest that the time has come to stop using Jesus's name which has divided us, and return to his work which will unite us.

—PIERRE CERESOLE.

Most of us think that the lives of saints are all trumped-up, but when we hear about modern saints it changes our minds.

Learning about people broadens your mind. I'd rather dramatize it than sit and write all lesson. You can take it in easier and see how people would react when it took place.

I like Religious Education/Drama a lot better than the way we did it at our Primary School. We used to sit there for half an hour each week while the teacher used to babble on and on never stopping to talk to us, so we forgot everything five minutes after she told it.

I like Religious Education/Drama so much and I only wish I could have a few more lessons a week. Since we have been doing Religious Education/Drama I have improved tremendously.

Drama shows what people's feelings are, with sitting in desks you just learn words.

—WRITTEN REPLIES FROM CHILDREN ON THEIR REACTIONS TO RELIGIOUS EDUCATION/DRAMA LESSONS.

1. INTRODUCTION

One of the most exciting educational advances to have taken place during the last decade is the growth of Creative Drama as a curriculum subject in an increasing number of schools. The use of drama as a means of expounding the Christian faith is an ancient one. The medieval church, with its miracle and mystery plays, used the medium to advantage encouraging the actors to improvise their own lines as they played out the great biblical sagas to enthralled audiences in towns and cities throughout the country. Learning became an enjoyable experience, a memorable respite from the back-breaking toil of a pre-mechanized society.

The Defiant Ones is intended as a supplement to the Religious Education syllabus in Secondary schools, by presenting, through drama, the biographies of a series of twentieth-century social workers and priests,—uncanonized 'saints'—who, by defying convention, apathy, corruption, and the prospect of a violent death, achieved, and are achieving, a better world for their fellow men to live in.

One of the objects of Religious Education must be to present children with the fact that there are people living in the world today who are far worse off than themselves and, more important still, that there are people prepared to do something about it; to show that saintliness is not just a quality found within the pages of the Bible, or among a select few who lived during the Middle Ages, but a living force that will flourish as long as man himself.

The problems that these 'Defiant Ones' are wrestling with

3

are the problems that will ultimately affect the lives of our children; the problems of hunger, disease, corruption in high places, apathy, forgiveness, cruelty, and oppression.

Each biography represents a modern illustration of Christ's counsel that we 'Love our neighbour as ourselves': Father Borrelli going out into the Neapolitan slums to rescue the poor, deprived scugnizzi; Father Pierre building homes for the poverty-stricken French refugees at the end of the Second World War; Danilo Dolci turning his back on a prosperous career as an architect in order to devote his life to feeding the hungry bandits of Western Sicily.

Drama has been chosen as the principal medium through which to explore the lives of these courageous men and women because children enjoy acting, and if the Religious Education lesson is to be meaningful it must also be pleasurable at the same time. Children are extremely active by nature and need very little encouragement to be up and out of their seats acting out a variety of roles as they strive to make sense of the world in which they live.

Play is a natural part of childhood and educational drama seeks to channel this natural spontaneous impulse into a controlled and worthwhile educational experience. Learning becomes an effortless process when the facts of a lesson are dramatized, and the information thus acquired is less likely to be forgotten than if taught by more conventional means. Drama gives children the opportunity to look at life from other people's points of view. Not only will they share Father Borrelli's decision to become a scugnizzo, but they will also become aware of the temptations that he will have to face as they change roles and become his superiors deliberating whether or not to grant him his wish. Similarly, they can switch from playing the parts of Dolci and his friends to play the Sicilian authorities who opposed him.

Through this type of dramatic role-playing children learn to look at life from differing points of view; and to be able to see another person's point of view, without necessarily agreeing with it, is one of the most desperate needs of our time, without which no dialogue is possible between opposing groups. To understand brings understanding. There can be no finer purpose for the Religious Education lesson. When a problem is first presented dramatically the ensuing discussion is always far livelier because of the personal involvement that has taken place, and it is possible to reach greater truths because the child's whole personality has been brought to bear upon the problem.

Drama can be one of the finest teaching aids that the teacher has at his command. In the words of a thirteen-year-old girl, 'It is more interesting to act a story than just talk and write about it. It is more interesting when we act it because it will stick in our minds more. When we grow up and somebody asks us what we think about a person, we will think of those we just talked and wrote about at school and we will remember how dull it was, and say, "Oh, I was not much interested in him, I think he was rather boring". But if we have acted his life, we will be able to say, "Yes, it was very interesting because I know what it felt like to be Dolci when he went on a hunger strike; because when we were acting scenes from his life I was pretending to be Dolci and I knew why he did it. If I were writing it all down I would just put down what I was told to and not get the real meaning of it at all".'

The layout of each biographical section follows the same pattern, beginning with a piece of research connected with the story. For example, a discovery of the differences between Roman Catholics and Communists is essential for an understanding of the conflict between Dolci and Don Zeno over the employment of communist workers at Don Zeno's Catholic Community at Nomadelfia. A reading list is included and it is hoped that as many of the books as possible are ordered for the children's use in order to supplement the information given here. The pictures and maps that they contain are invaluable for a full understanding of the 'Defiant Ones' and the social conditions under which they are working.

Then follows an improvisation which seeks to establish a contact between a major event in the lives of each of the characters and a parallel occurrence that could take place within the children's own experience. As a preface to the work on Father Borrelli and the scugnizzi, the children are asked to imagine themselves as scugnizzi within their own social surroundings before going on to read about the conditions in Naples.

The work must always be related to the children's own experiences. In the argument between Dolci and his father over his refusal to stay on at University and take his degree it is useful to ask the children what plans their own parents have for their future careers. 'My Dad wants me to be a farmer', 'Mine wants me to be a mechanic'. Then ask them to imagine the situation at home if they themselves told their parents that they were not going to sit for their GCE or CSE examinations, but were leaving school to be come labourers on a building site, thus giving up their chance of going on to agricultural college or university.

The greater part of the book consists of a series of improvisations based upon the more dramatic episodes in the lives of the 'Defiant Ones' and linked by a running commentary. Few children care to work on an improvisation solely for their own enjoyment; therefore, they must be given an opportunity of showing what they have done to their friends. There are two ways of doing this, each involving the children working in groups. Either the introductory linking material is read by the teacher or members of the class, who then split up into groups and practise the same improvisation; or alternatively, each group can be given a different improvisation (providing that they are taken in a logical sequence) which they rehearse and then present to the rest of the class, one member of the group introducing the scene by reading the preceding commentary. This system is recommended if time is short as it takes longer to work through the material if they are all engaged upon the same scene.

Some discretion is needed if the first method is employed. Children find it interesting at first to see how others have tackled the work, but the idea of watching 4 or 5 groups performing the identical scene soon palls. Therefore, some method of selection is necessary. One group could be chosen each lesson to show their improvisation, followed in the next lesson by another group, and so on. Unfortunately, children would soon learn the system and those not presenting their plays, realizing that they are only practising for their own enjoyment, would soon lose interest and standards would begin to decline. In addition, children are always changing their friends and the composition of the groups would not remain static each week. It is more satisfactory for a part of each group's work to be shown each lesson.

Taking 'The new boy' on page 29 as an example: Group A could show the new boy being questioned by the scugnizzi; Group B could take over at the point where the gang switch their attention to Borrelli and seek to find out where he goes during the day; Group C could show the arrival of the boy's father; and Group D, the father dragging the boy away to the amusement of the scugnizzi. Several of the improvisations are too short to allow this to happen, but in that case there will be time for several scenes to be shown in one lesson.

The children can be left entirely on their own to present the scenes as they think fit, or each improvisation can be read and discussed before the children go into their groups. Younger children are keen to get on with the acting and become bored by too much discussion, but with older children, who are developing a feeling for characterization, time spent in discussing the work pays dividends. In 'You've brought us all this way for that!', page 72, what kind of people are Gaspar, Chicot, and Auguste? What personal tragedies brought them to Pierre? What kind of a maid is Bertha? Aloof? Shy? Friendly? Is Madame Reyner eccentric? Does she really believe that the chipped fruit-dish will be of value to Pierre?

Male parts predominate and, as most schools are now co-educational, girls will automatically have to play men's parts. Fortunately, they do not seem to mind, especially the younger girls; it is far more difficult to get boys to take women's parts. Nevertheless, the Religious Education/Drama lesson must be a fluid affair and the teacher must be prepared to change characters to suit the temperaments of the children taking part. There is no reason why the scugnizzi gangs should not be made up entirely of girls, if, by doing so, the girls are made to feel that the work has more relevance.

There are times when the whole class can take part in the same improvisation under the guidance of the teacher. Many of the scugnizzi scenes can be treated in this way. Dolci's trial also calls for a large cast of jurymen, witnesses, court officials, police officers and members of the public. Another example is 'Borgo di Dio—temporarily closed' page 127.

No written exercises have been included, but the work lends itself particularly well to free-verse composition especially after the children have acted out some of the strongly emotional scenes, such as the death of Justina Barretta's baby, page 109. Here are some specimens from the class-room:

Dirty, black, animal-like and wet.

Not possible.

The need for justice and peace of mind.
Sick, thin and weary,
Full of death.
The want of good homes and work.
Sadness and poverty unceasing.

A SECOND-YEAR BOY.

Dolci's hunger strike:

He began to hunger.
All hope had gone:
His body had begun to shrivel
And his face was pallid now.
I felt that my friend was in Hell's fires,
And the devil had begun to torture him.
Oh, God, those damned authorities.

After days of hellish torture,
The authorities came into the stinking hole
In all their posh regalia.
They handed him three crisp forms,
Danilo signed them with his limp hand.
Everyone cheered.

A SECOND-YEAR BOY.

And after two weeks of being a scugnizzo:

> *I'm tired and I'm lonely,*
> *I'm ragged, dirty too.*
> *My pals feel all the same,*
> *I spend my days hunting for cigarette ends.*
> *I'll sprawl upon the gutter*
> *And cough the night away*
> *My stomach feels so empty*
> *For I've had nothing to eat at all.*
>
> *I try to earn a living*
> *And hardly succeed.*
> *Stale bread I'll eat, or even orange rind,*
> *It's all the same to me—I don't mind.*
> *My life is hard—I toil away,*
> *I'm very sick.*
> *By day I'm hot, dirty, sticky,*
> *At night I'm cold, dirty and lonely,*
> *But do I mind—no!*

A FIRST-YEAR GIRL.

Few props are needed; some chairs and a desk or two will suffice. Children are highly inventive with even the minimum of material available. A few chairs placed side by side serve as a bed; tables turned upside down for fishing-boats.

The principal difficulty encountered in attempting to dramatize the lives of pacifists such as Dolci is the way in which children find it extremely difficult to take orders from those who are physically weaker than themselves. When the police, armed with guns, burst into Borgo to close it down, the children playing Dolci and his friends may want to resist. Children have no fear whatever of imaginary guns, and the situation has to be related to their own experience before they can play it as intended. They will quickly see the parallel between the entry of a headmaster to quieten a rowdy class and the arrival of the police to intimidate Dolci and his friends. But their difficulty in accepting a role of passive resistance will only be overcome through discussion of the motives that inspire it and through a change of roles, so that the police play Dolci and his friends and vice versa.

The teaching of drama can be one of the most worthwhile subjects that a teacher can take. Children are capable of playing scenes of quite powerful emotional intensity, and it is one of drama's greatest boons that it is not always the most intelligent children who excel. Drama is something that everyone can take part in, and achieve satisfaction from.

And the end result of this work? Christ's words, 'As you did it to one of the least of these my brethren you did it to me', can be rephrased to read: 'As you have caught the spirit of Don Borrelli, the Abbé Pierre and Danilo Dolci, you have caught the spirit of me'. God is found, not only in the pages of the Bible or during the morning assembly, but also in the low-class streets of Naples, the hovels of Paris and the slums of Trappetto. When all the 'thievings' and 'killings' have been forgotten, the spirit that inspired these modern saints will live on in the children's memories providing them with a yardstick for the rest of their lives.

Note on donations:

At the end of each study, one way in which the pupils may wish to respond is by organizing a collection in aid of the work they have been investigating. For this purpose relevant addresses have been supplied. Such collections could, of course, only be made if this were consistent with the school's policy on this matter. At the same time it should be stressed that this course is not intended to draw attention to these particular men and situations at the expense of the many other similar causes, some of which might well be more urgent and topical at the time of study. An equally appropriate response would be to send donations to one of these.

BIBLIOGRAPHY

ADLAND D. E. *Group Drama* (Longmans)
BRUCE Violet R. and TOOKE Joan D. *Lord of the Dance* (Pergamon)
COURTNEY Richard. *Play, Drama and Thought* (Cassell)
HAGGERTY J. *Please, Miss Can I Play God?* (Methuen)
H.M.S.O. *Drama*
HODGSON J. and RICHARDS E. *Improvisation* (Methuen)
JOHNSON H. Findlay. *The Dramatic Method of Teaching* (James Nisbet and Co. Ltd. 1910)

2. FATHER BORRELLI
AND THE HOUSE OF THE
SPINNING TOPS

Go out into the highways and hedges and compel them to come in, that my house may be filled.

ST. LUKE **14**.23

PRELIMINARY WORK

1. Draw a map of Italy showing Naples and Rome.

2. Find out as much as you can about Naples from travel books and encyclopaedias, and then write an essay illustrating your work with pictures from magazines and holiday brochures.

3. Try to obtain the following books for your school library; they each contain information about Father Borrelli and the scugnizzi.

BORRELLI Don and THORNE Anthony *A Street Lamp and the Stars* (Peter Davies). This is Father Borrelli's own story.

DAVY Cyril *The Santi Story* (Epworth Press, London). This is an account of how a Methodist minister, Riccardo Santi, together with his three talented sons, like Father Borrelli, have spent their lives helping the poor people of Naples.

OLIVER Mark *Five Spinning Tops of Naples* (J. M. Dent and Sons Ltd.). This is a novel which tells the story of two brothers, Ferdinando and Orlando Caffarelli, who run away from home and join the scugnizzi.

(Various Authors) *Heroes of Our Time* (Gollancz).

WEST Morris *Children of the Sun* (Heinemann). This is the story of Father Borrelli and his work amongst the scugnizzi.

4. You can borrow a film about the work of Father Borrelli called *Naples, the Anonymous* from:

The House of the Urchins Fund, 19 Rodger Drive, Rutherglen, Glasgow.

IMPROVISATION

Imagine that both your parents have been killed and you have no relatives. You make your way to the nearest city centre and there you join a group of homeless children like yourself, who have formed themselves into a gang with the strongest as the leader. Because you have no money to buy food you begin to steal, not in a big way—no bank robberies —just a tin of meat from a market stall, a sheet from a clothes line to sell in a junk shop, or a bottle of milk from a doorstep. You sleep out in the streets at night, huddled in shop door-ways to keep yourselves warm, with newspapers for sheets and the cold steps for a mattress.

Now go into groups and make up a play showing *one* incident that took place while you were living this kind of life. End your play with one of the gang saying:

I wouldn't like to go through that again'.

Now come together as a class and talk amongst yourselves about your adventures. Several of you might like to tell the rest of the class what happened.

THE SCUGNIZZI

Scugnizzo is an Italian work meaning 'spinning-top' (plural *scugnizzi*) and is the name given to over 3000 Neapolitan children aged between 8 and 18, who, for one reason or another, have run away from home and now live by their wits, and what they can steal, in the back-street slums (the *Bassi*) of Naples. Many of them are sick and diseased suffering from asthma, trachoma, ringworm, scabies, swollen lips, and rack-ing coughs that bring up blood. The effects of these can so stunt their normal growth that some 16-year-old scugnizzi have the bodies of very young children. The terribly hard life that they lead has made them stubborn and distrustful of strangers.

There are two kinds of scugnizzi: the professionals who have no one to care for them and are completely on their own; and the amateurs, the latch-key children whose parents allow them to stay out all night if they wish. They mix with the wrong kind of people and before their parents realize what is happening the rot has set in—they, too, have become scugnizzi.

The professionals turn scugnizzi for many reasons. Their parents cannot afford to look after them, or one parent has married again and the child's stepfather, or stepmother, is so hostile that he is forced to leave home. Many come from broken homes where the mother cannot cope, and the children have to seek a living elsewhere. In some cases, the child is the only wage-earner and, realizing that he is being exploited, he eventually breaks with the family and branches out on his own—too young to stand the heavy weight of responsibility pressing down upon him. Others come from decent homes, but a fascination for the seamier side of life drags them away from home. Some even hitch-hike from Rome, 150 miles away, sleeping in ditches along the way.

The scugnizzi form themselves into gangs numbering from six to twenty members. The leader is usually an older boy chosen for his strength, his ability to organize, his cunning in avoiding the police, his skill as a thief, his influence among the other gangs, and the useful contacts that he has made in the Neapolitan underworld.

In a scugnizzi gang there is 'work' for everyone, even the youngest, who are sent begging for food at convents, barracks, hotels, and restaurants, and for cast-off clothes from private houses; they always arouse more pity from the general public than their older companions. The youngsters also play a vitally important part in the 'snow gathering'. In Naples, the housewives hang their sheets out to dry across the alleyways, from house to house. On washdays, groups of scugnizzi find a deserted alley, and then form themselves into a human pyramid under a washing line. The youngest member of the gang climbs up onto his friend's shoulders and unpegs the sheets, which are then spirited away and sold on the 'flea market'.

The scugnizzi spend most of their time collecting cigarette butts (*spiniellos*). These are picked up in cinemas, night-clubs, bars and gambling dens, and at bus and tram stops. The tobacco is removed, parcelled up, and sold for anything up to 100 lire a package (500 lire is approximately 6*s*. 8*d*.) to the local workmen. If a scugnizzo has been exceptionally lucky he can earn from 1300 to 1600 lire for one kilogramme (1000 grammes) of this sticky 'second hand' tobacco; but it takes 4 butt ends to yield the equivalent amount of tobacco for one cigarette, so, in order to pick up 1000 grammes, he would have to bend down over 4000 times! The butts thrown away by the American sailors down on the water front bring in an extra 200 lire a kilogramme because of their richer tobacco. Butts which have been stubbed out in an ashtray are better than those which have burned away to ash in the gutter.

The sale of used tobacco is illegal in Italy as the State holds the monopoly on the sale of cigarettes. The police are constantly on the look-out for the young tobacco salesmen who let out a special whistle, reminiscent of a factory siren, to warn their friends when a police search is in progress. As soon as this whistle is heard all the scugnizzi in the area take off their shoes and race for the darkest most inaccessible alleyways of the *Bassi*. The growing popularity of the filter-tip cigarette with its worthless butt is now slowly strangling the trade.

The scugnizzi are not basically thieves and pickpockets. Some, admittedly, will steal from Church poor-boxes, the alms from a beggar or food from the market stalls, but only if they are hungry; they will never plan a robbery. It has to be a spontaneous act—on the spur of the moment.

THERE'S A HOLE IN MY POCKET

CHARACTERS: *Franchetiello—a scugnizzo*
Members of the gang
The owner of the fruit stall

SCENE: A fruit stall on the market.

1. The stallholder is calling out 'Juicy oranges!' 'Crisp, fresh lettuces' etc.

2. A gang of scugnizzi walk up to the stallholder and hold him in conversation (choose any subject you like).

3. While the stallholder is distracted by the gang, Franchetiello, one of the scugnizzi, moves close to the stall and begins slipping lemons, red peppers, and curly lettuces into his trouser pockets, which have large holes in the linings and are tied at the turn-ups with pieces of string. The fruit falls through the holes and is caught in the legs of his baggy trousers.

4. His trouser-legs grow thicker and thicker as he pushes more and more fruit and vegetables through the holes in his pockets.

Now finish this scene yourselves. Does the stallholder catch Frenchetiello? What do the rest of the gang do?

WHO'S KNOCKED MY DISPLAY OVER?

CHARACTERS: *Flea—a scugnizzo*
The rest of the gang
The owner of the meat stall

SCENE: A meat stall on the Naples market. A large pyramid of American tinned meat stands at the front of the stall.

1. A crowd of scugnizzi walk past the stall and Flea, accidently (or on purpose!) knocks one of the bottom tins of the pyramid and the whole pile falls crashing to the ground. Flea picks up one of the tins and dives under the stall. He opens the tin and begins to eat the contents.

2. The stallholder bends down and begins to pick up his scattered tins of meat.

3. The rest of the gang stand by laughing as they watch the stallholder trying to rebuild his fallen display. One of the gang suddenly discovers that Flea is missing. They search for him and eventually find him sitting under the stall finishing off his tin of stolen meat.

What happens next? Does the stallholder catch Flea?

LAP A PINTA MILKA DAY

CHARACTERS: *Flea—a scugnizzo*
A milkman
Householders

SCENE: Early morning in a respectable quarter of Naples. The milkman has just been on his rounds and has left 3 bottles of milk on the doorstep of a large detached house.

1. Flea walks down the street. Seeing the milk, he grabs one of the bottles and runs off down the street with it. Rounding a corner he falls straight into the arms of the returning milkman.

2. The milkman is furious and beats Flea almost senseless. Flea, still clutching the bottle, squeals for mercy. Windows open in the neighbouring houses as the occupants try to find out what is happening. The milkman is far too angry to reply.

3. Flea drops the bottle; it breaks, and the milk runs away into the gutter. The milkman knocks Flea down and storms off.

4. Rather than waste the precious milk, Flea begins to lap it up, like a dog, until it becomes too muddy to drink. The householders are disgusted. Angrily they tell him to go away 'This is a respectable neighbourhood'. Flea slinks away.

THE POSTEGGIA

(*The scugnizzi are also past masters at the art of making money by false pretences.*

Go into your groups and make up a play based on the following incident.)

CHARACTERS: *A rich American tourist*   *Lame Duck*
              Wooden Head   *Mangy*
              Louse   *Fatty*
              Whiskers   *Little Mouse*
              One-armed   *Tarzan (strong)*
              Cheese Head (stupid)   *Drain Rat*
              Big Head   *Chink Eyes*

(These are scugnizzi nicknames. Use them yourselves or make up new ones of your own.)

SCENE: A gang of scugnizzi are standing on the corner of the Garibaldi Piazza near the station.

1. A new boy has joined the gang and one of the group is telling him how easy it is to get money out of the rich tourists by playing a confidence trick on them known as the *Posteggia*. Having bought 10 lire's worth of Citrate of Magnesium, the scugnizzo takes an envelope out of his pocket, taps out the powder onto the palm of his hand and then waits for a rich tourist to come along.

2. 'Quick! There's a rich American coming!' shouts one of the gang. The boy swallows the powder and walks out into the middle of the square.

3. Suddenly, he begins to foam at the mouth. He falls to the ground writhing and twitching, holding his stomach, and groaning in agony.

4. The American bends over him and asks what is wrong. The rest of the gang rush out and explain that the boy is very ill and needs medicine, but they have no money. The American puts his hand into his pocket and takes out a handful of change which he gives to the leader of the gang.

5. The gang rush away carrying the 'sick' boy with them. Around the corner, and out of sight of the American, the boy miraculously recovers and they quarrel furiously amongst themselves over the share-out of the money.

At the end of each day the scugnizzi collect waste paper and sacks for their bedding and make their way to a sheltered doorway or the ventilator grills set into the pavement over a bakery where the warm air helps them to withstand the cold Neapolitan night. They bring with them a rusty tin full of holes that serves as a stove, and a small quantity of charcoal bought during the day. The youngsters keep the fire going with dried orange peel, cork, pieces of wood, cardboard and rubber soles. They snuggle down around the stove which usually goes out in the early hours of the morning through lack of fuel. Sleep is difficult; they are kept awake by the fleas and lice (the *volante*—the 'flying squad' as they call them) and the rats. Some disentangle themselves from the mass of sleeping bodies and chafe their hands and stamp their feet in an attempt to keep warm.

The authorities consider them a blight on the landscape. The rich foreign tourists are shown the splendours of Naples— the sweeping horseshoe bay, the craggy coast of Sorrento, and the lovely Isle of Capri, shimmering in the distance across the Oxford blue waters of the bay, the Art galleries and museums, the magnificent Opera House; but no one invites the tourist to view the other Naples, the Naples of the *Bassi*— the home of the scugnizzi.

Up to 1950, the Santi family and a handful of dedicated Salvation Army workers were the only people to care about the scugnizzi; and then a small Roman Catholic priest called Don Borrelli decided that he too must try to do something for these desperate children. But what?

Now make up your own scugnizzi plays using the following titles to help you:

1. *Trouble at bedtime.*
2. *Where have all my fag ends gone?*
3. *The beggar at the Barracks.*
4. *The new leader.*
5. *The stranger from Rome.*
6. *I didn't want to be a scugnizzo.*

Write a poem about a scugnizzo. Begin it with one of the following lines:

1. *I spend my days collecting fag ends,*
   I spend my nights huddled round the baker's drain.

2. *Scugnizzi are miserable,*
   Scugnizzi are poor.

3. *My puffed-up eyes, my puffed-up lips,*
   I am alone all day picking up butts.

DON MARIO BORRELLI

Don Mario Borrelli was born in the dockland area of Naples in 1922. His father was a silver gilder who worked at home carrying out repairs for the large city jewellers. Money was scarce and to help out young Mario went to work for a local barber, bringing in drinks for the customers as they waited to have their hair cut.

One of the regular customers was a Roman Catholic priest called Don Nobilione, and, for something to say as he paid for his coffee, he asked 13-year-old Mario what he wanted to be when he grew up. 'A priest, sir,' replied the boy. Don Nobilione pointed out that a barber's shop was hardly the training-ground for the priesthood. He took Mario home to ask his mother if she could afford to send Mario back to school. But there was little money and Mrs. Borrelli could not afford to finance her son's further education. Don Nobilione, sensing Mario's obvious disappointment, agreed to pay for the boy's schooling. But at the end of the first year he could no longer afford to assist his young student. Undeterred, Mario managed to persuade his mother to pay his fees. He knew that he had to succeed at school. If he slipped from the position that he had gained at the top of the class, he would have to go back to the barber's shop. Life was hard. He knew what it was to struggle along with little money, while his clothes grew thinner and shabbier each day.

Success at school led to a seven-year course of training for the priesthood and in 1946 he was ordained a Roman Catholic priest.

With his boundless energy and enthusiasm, one job was not sufficient for Mario. He accepted four appointments: as interpreter to the Holy Year Committee, as a priest in charge of a travelling chapel, as a teacher, and as a youth club leader in his spare time.

For a while he was delegated to a party of tough charcoal-burners in a remote part of Italy. It was here that he had an experience that was to have a marked effect upon his future actions. Believing that a priest can get closer to his congregation if he becomes like one of them, he took off his priest's habit and dressed as an ordinary workman. He hired a mule and gained the confidence and respect of these isolated charcoal-burners by supplying them with food and tobacco.

On his first visit he suggested that some of them might like to attend Mass down in the village the following Sunday. As he celebrated the Mass in his priestly vestments he saw that some of his customers were in the congregation. They would recognize him as the man with the mule. Would they feel let down? Deceived? He had no need to worry; they accepted him as eagerly as a priest as they had done when he was a travelling salesman.

Back in Naples, he began to think seriously about the scugnizzi, those children 'who, through no fault of their own have never had the time, or opportunity, to remain innocent'. An audacious plan began to form in his mind. In order to help them, he must get to know them—find out their needs; but the black soutane (cassock) and the shovel hat that he wore would be a barrier between them. He had dressed as a charcoal-burner in order to mix more freely with the charcoal-burners; might he not also dress as a scugnizzo in order to be closer to them? He could still teach during the day, and be a scugnizzo at night.

But there were obstacles in his path, not least of which were his own superiors: the Monsignori (priests) and Cardinals of the Roman Catholic Church. Could he persuade them to agree to his plan?

(*Go into discussion groups and make a list of all the reasons you can think of in favour of Mario becoming a scugnizzo; then write down all the objections that his superiors might make when they heard of his plans.*)

To help strengthen his case he toured the streets with Salvatore, a photographer, taking pictures of the scugnizzi in all their poverty, misery, and distress.

A PRIEST! LIVING LIKE A SCUGNIZZO!

(*To get his wish Mario had to persuade three Monsignori and a Cardinal.*)

CHARACTERS: *Monsignor A* (*Mario's superior*)
Mario

SCENE: The house of Monsignor A.

1. Mario knocks on the Monsignor's study door and the Monsignor calls to him to come in.

(*Put all the arguments that you thought up in your discussion groups into this scene.*)

2. Mario, you have got to convince this man that what you are doing is right; remember to show him your photographs, and don't forget to tell him of the pathetic scenes that you saw as you toured the stinking alleyways of the *Bassi* with Salvatore.

3. Monsignor A, this is an unheard of thing that Mario is suggesting. Don't give in too easily.

4. End the scene with Monsignor A promising to have a word with Monsignor B.

Now change partners and go through the scene again, this time with Mario imagining that he is speaking to Monsignor B. End the scene with Monsignor B promising to have a word with Monsignor C.

Change partners again and finally improvise the scene with Monsignor C. End the scene with Monsignor C promising to have a word with the Cardinal.

Three Monsignori to convince, and finally a conversation with Cardinal Ascalesi, Archbishop of Naples and Primate of the Mezzogiorno, and Mario's wish was granted. They were allowing him to become a scugnizzo. The Cardinal gave his blessing:

'May Jesus bless you, my son! And protect you too. For there will be so many dangers—so many'.

Mario went out in search of a scugnizzi gang that he could join.

CAN I JOIN YOU?

CHARACTERS: *A Salvation Army Officer*
Members of the gang
Fatty—the leader
Mario.

SCENE: A street in the *Bassi*. A table stands on the pavement spread out with slices of bread, pieces of chocolate, and mugs of hot milk. A Salvation Army Officer is handing out refreshments to a group of scugnizzi—all eager to be served first.

1. Mario enters. He is wearing a pair of dirty, threadbare trousers, an old shirt that he found in a dustbin, a dirty old cap and a frayed scarf. One shoe is larger than the other and they are both laced up with pieces of string. He sits down on the pavement. The group turn to face the intruder.

2. Fatty, the leader, slouches across to Mario and pulls his large cap down over his eyes.
    'Who are you?' he drawls.

3. Mario stands up and spits right into Fatty's face.
    'That's who I am'.

4. The scugnizzi are silent, watching, wondering what Fatty will do next.

5. Mario knew enough about the scugnizzi to realise that Fatty would go for his knife.
    Quick as a flash, Mario grabs him by his right sleeve to stop him seizing his weapon. He thrusts his free hand into his own pocket.
    'What's the matter with you? I've got a right to a bit of warmth, haven't I. Same as anyone else? And something to eat too, and who's stopping me?'

5. Like a Western gunfighter, Mario has beaten Fatty to the draw, and Fatty accepts his boldness. Little did he realize that Mario had no knife—he was bluffing. Fatty takes his razor-blade out of his pocket and offers it to Mario.

'I'd have carved you. I'd have carved you so your own mother wouldn't have known you. But you got your hand in your pocket before I did. So, here you are'.

6. Mario accepts Fatty's razor-blade and introduces himself. (Be careful here, Mario, don't give too much away). Then Fatty presents the various members of the gang.

Mario had become a scugnizzo. During the day he carried out his teaching commitments and at night he changed into his dirty clothes and roamed the streets in search of his friends. If the members of the gang ever asked him what he did during the day he would usually ignore the question, tell them a funny story, make them laugh, and his absences during the day would be forgotten. But on one particular night they became more insistent in their enquiries.

THE NEW BOY

CHARACTERS: *Mario*
The new boy
Members of the gang
The new boy's father

SCENE: A pavement by a bakery wall. It is evening.

1. A new boy has joined the gang and they are questioning him about his past. Where does he come from? Has he any parents? Why did he run away from home? (*Make up your*

own answers, boy.) But it is the same old story, they have heard it all many times before.

2. One of the gang asks Mario where he disappears to during the day. He tries to laugh it off, but the others join in. None of them have ever seen Mario during the day. Where does he go? How does he spend his time? Mario tries to answer their questions truthfully without giving the game away; but the situation is becoming difficult.

3. Suddenly, a man rushes up to the gang. He is in a violent temper. He seizes hold of the new boy and beats him unmercifully, explaining to the scugnizzi that the boy is his son who ran away from home two days ago. He has been out searching for him ever since.

4. He drags the sobbing lad away. The gang laughingly discuss what has happened. Mario's daytime disappearances are once again forgotten.

GO AND MAKE A NOISE SOMEWHERE ELSE!

(*The gang was continually being moved on by Neapolitans who objected to gangs of scugnizzi living and sleeping on the pavements outside their shops and houses.*)

CHARACTERS: *Mangy*
                      Members of the gang
                      Woman with a broom
                      Little Mouse
                      A rich tourist

SCENE 1:   Outside a private house in the *Bassi*.
SCENE 2:   Inside a derelict house on the sea front.

SCENE 3: A street.
It is night time.

1. Members of the gang are teasing Mangy, and trying to pull off his cap, which is stuck to the scabs on his head. Their noise wakes up a woman sleeping in the nearby house. She comes out with a broom and chases them away.

2. Further down the street they stop for breath. They are tired of being chased from bakehouse to bakehouse, from doorway to doorway. Someone suggests spending the night in one of the derelict houses down by the sea front. No one is likely to move them on down there. They make their way down to the promenade.

3. They find a deserted house and go inside. It is in the last stages of collapse. Little Mouse goes on ahead. Suddenly, there is the sound of falling masonry and a cry. They rush into the next room and find Little Mouse trapped under a heavy beam. Part of the ceiling has fallen in. They manage to lift the debris clear and find that Mouse's leg has been severely crushed by the falling timbers.

4. They carry him out into the street. A rich tourist is walking towards them. They stop him and ask for help . . . money; but, unfortunately, for Little Mouse, the Tourist has been told of the confidence tricks played by the scugnizzi. He will give them nothing. He walks on.

What do you think happens to Little Mouse? Improvise your own ending. Remember that if you bring Mario into this he must not reveal that he is a priest—it would ruin all his plans.

Mario soon realized that what the scugnizzi really needed was a place of their own, somewhere to sleep, a place where they could get a meal, a place where they could be free to do as they pleased, within limits, a place where there were few rules, a place that they could call home.

With the idea that one day such a home would need helpers, Mario recruited Don Spada, another priest and a friend of his student days, and Vittorio, a teacher, who understood the scugnizzi and their problems.

The three of them managed to persuade the Roman Catholic authorities to allow them the use of a derelict bombed-out church as a centre for the scugnizzi. Don Spada and Vittorio began the work of renovation, helped by Mario in his spare time!

They obtained blankets, and sacks which they stuffed with straw for use as mattresses. When the need for proper mattresses arose they bought themselves a hand-cart and earned the money to pay for them by going from door to door collecting old iron to sell to the local scrap merchants. As time when on and the business grew they exchanged the barrow for a donkey and cart, and eventually, as their profits increased, they bought a lorry in which to collect the junk.

Mario felt that it was too soon to give up his life as a scugnizzo and reveal to his friends that he was really a priest, and yet he longed to find out how the scugnizzi would take to their rapidly developing club-house at the old church of the Materdei. As an experiment he asked Vittorio to find a scugnizzi gang and see if he could persuade some of them to give up their life on the streets in exchange for the comforts of a place of their own.

WHY DON'T YOU GIVE UP THIS LIFE?

CHARACTERS: *Vittorio*
Members of the gang
Cheese Head
Don Spada
Mario

SCENE 1: The Street of the Two Lepers.

1. A group of scugnizzi are discussing the art of pickpocketing.

2. Vittorio joins them and sits listening to their conversation. They are young ones, unlikely to challenge him as Mario was challenged by Fatty. During a lull in their conversation, Vittorio tells them that he once saw a pickpocket, and a lad who was obviously learning the business, sidle up to a rich-looking man on a tram. The man had a bulging wallet sticking out of his back pocket. The lad produced a knife ready to cut out the pocket and snatch the wallet away. Unfortunately for both of them, the tram gave a lurch at the very moment that the lad was using his knife and it went in further than he had anticipated. The man gave a cry of pain and the pickpockets made off in the confusion, minus the wallet. The scugnizzi laugh hilariously.

3. Vittorio tells them that he knows of a place that would be just right for them; where food and shelter are provided free of charge and no one chases them away.

4. The scugnizzi, always suspicious of strangers, tell Vittorio that they are quite happy where they are. Only one boy, Cheese Head, takes up Vittorio's offer.

SCENE 2: The old church, two days later.

1. Cheese Head is alone in the old church. He walks up and down. There is nothing to do. He is bored.

2. Don Spada comes in and Cheese Head immediately begins to grumble. He misses his friends.

3. Don Spada tries to point out the advantages of living in the old church. Doesn't Cheese Head enjoy the food? Doesn't he like sleeping with a roof over his head?

4. Yes! Yes! He likes these things, but there is no one to talk to; it is almost as bad as solitary confinement in the House of Correction on the grey stone island of Procida.

5. Cheese Head walks out. Don Spada tries to stop him, but it is hopeless. He has made up his mind to leave.

6. Don Spada sits down. He feels that they have failed.

7. Mario puts his head round the door and asks if it is safe for him to come in—he does not wish to be recognized by Cheese Head.

8. Don Spada tells him that Cheese Head has left. Mario tells him not to worry. One boy has run away, but the day will come when the old church will be full of scugnizzi, all happy to be living there. Don Spada hopes that he is right.

Weeks pass. The old church gradually began to take on a fresh character and Mario felt that the time had come for another attempt at persuading the scugnizzi to come in off the streets. Pasquale, another priest, and Salvatore, the photographer, were chosen to talk to the gang. Mario was there too—as a scugnizzo. After a great deal of argument Pasquale and Salvatore at last persuaded several members of the gang to come back with them to the old church. They knew that once they could induce a few of the boys to stay on then the news would travel and others would come too.

The scugnizzi took to their new way of life; some returned to the streets, but most of them were soon back again after a few days. The food, the beds and, what was more important, honest work—collecting the scrap iron to sell to pay for their keep—these were far more attractive propositions than selling used tobacco and living in the dark alleyways of the *Bassi*. They were learning to become respectable and self-respecting citizens.

Mario continued his nightly visits; but life was hard and there were many dangers.

WHAT SORT OF SCUGNIZZO ARE YOU?

CHARACTERS: *Boy from an older gang*
Michele—a member of an older gang
Mario

SCENE 1: The Vicolo die Biricchini—the street of the villains.

1. Michele enters. He is very drunk. He staggers down the street, trips over, and falls into a drunken sleep in the gutter.

2. Mario and an older scugnizzo meet over Michele's sleeping figure. The older boy is out to rob Michele and he tells Mario to go away. He saw Michele first.

3. Mario tells him that he has no intention of robbing Michele. The older boy then accuses Mario of being a police squealer. Mario hotly denies that he is anything of the sort.

4. The older boy searches Michele's pockets and takes out his cigarettes and his money, putting them in his own pocket. He

takes off Michele's boots. Mario is powerless to do anything about it. This is the law of the alley, any scugnizzo would do the same. If cigarettes, or boots, or money, are handed to you on a plate, as it were, then you would be a fool not to take them.

5. The older boy advises Mario not to be around when Michele wakes up. Without boots, and suffering from a hangover, Michele can still be a very nasty character. They both leave.

6. Michele wakes up, feels for his cigarettes.

A NARROW ESCAPE

CHARACTERS: *Mario*
A Nightwatchman

SCENE: Another street.

1. Mario is walking down the street. Suddenly, he hears the click of a safety catch being released on a gun, and a voice challenges him to stop where he is. It is a nightwatchman. He tells Mario that he is taking him to the police as he overheard him talking with some other scugnizzi, and he is certain that they are planning a robbery in the neighbourhood.

2. Mario tells him that he is a priest. (*How does Mario convince the nightwatchman?*) He tells him of the work that he is doing among the scugnizzi and makes him promise that he will not tell anyone about it. The watchman is most apologetic and tells Mario that it was fortunate for him that he did not attempt to run away when he was challenged. If he had done

so the watchman would have had no hesitation in shooting him in the legs.

Mario could reveal his true identity when there were no other scugnizzi around; but what happens when he comes into conflict with authority once more—this time with his friends?

SHORT CUT

CHARACTERS: *Whiskers*
Louse
Mario
Guards
An Officer

SCENE 1:   The railway lines.

1. Mario, Whiskers, and Louse, are taking a short cut across the railway lines. They are challenged by one of the city guards, dressed in a white uniform, a revolver in his holster, and carrying a truncheon nearly 2 feet long. They start to run away. The guard releases the safety-catch on his revolver. Mario calls to the others to stop. The guard will shoot if they continue to run away.

2. The guard questions Mario because he is the oldest. He asks him what they are doing on the railway lines. Mario tells him that they are taking a short cut, but the guard does not believe him. He feels that they are up to no good and he wants to know the truth. He knocks Mario down and hits him across the legs with his truncheon. He asks Mario again what they are doing on the railway lines. Mario repeatedly

tells him that they are only taking a short cut. The guard beats him again with his truncheon.

3. Other guards appear and Mario and his friends are marched off to the police barracks.

SCENE 2: At the Police Barracks.

1. Mario, Whiskers, and Louse are locked up in one of the cells. They are all feeling miserable, especially Mario, who has to be free by morning in order to teach his class. A guard walks by. Mario calls him over and asks to be allowed to speak to the Officer in charge. (*What reasons could Mario give for this? They will have to be convincing; the guard would not dare to disturb his superiors for anything of a trivial nature.*)

2. The guard takes Mario to see the officer. Mario reveals that he is a Roman Catholic Priest (*again how does he do this?*) and tells the Officer of the work that he is doing among the scugnizzi. The officer is most apologetic and orders Mario's instant release. Mario asks for Whiskers and Louse to be released at the same time.

3. The three scugnizzi walk out of the barracks together. As they make their way down the street Whiskers and Louse are very curious to know why they have been released so quickly. They want to know what Mario said to the Officer. What explanation does Mario give? Improvise your own ending.

It was becoming more and more difficult for Mario to keep his true identity from the scugnizzi. One of the priests inadvertently referred to him as 'Father' in front of some of the boys at the old church. Fortunately, the boys did not follow this up.

Mario learned that many of his young scugnizzi friends were drifting away from the district and joining a gang of older boys, more corrupt and hardened in their ways than anyone Mario had dealt with so far. Their leader was a tram-worker called Ciccillo. Mario realized that in order to save his boys he must first win over Ciccillo.

CLEAR OFF!

CHARACTERS: *Ciccillo—the leader of the gang*
Members of his gang
Mario

SCENE 1: A scugnizzi fire blazes in an old rusty bucket on the pavement. Members of the gang, including Ciccillo, are huddled around it.

1. Mario walks towards them. He lights a cigarette and draws nearer to the fire. He senses their hostility towards him. He is a stranger and all strangers are suspect. He bids them 'Good evening!' No one answers. Perhaps he is a police squealer.

2. Ciccillo stands up and slouches over to Mario.
Ciccillo: What do you want?
Mario: Only a bit of fire.
Ciccillo: There's fire all over Naples. Why pick on ours?
Mario: Well, somebody told me I could sleep here.
Ciccillo: Who told you?
Mario: I can't remember.
Ciccillo: I'll give you something to remember.

Ciccillo attacks Mario savagely, driving him away. Mario wards off the blows as best he can.

Mario's painfully unsuccessful attempt to win over Ciccillo did not deter him from returning the following evening to try again. Unknown to him, Salvatore had heard of his failure with Ciccillo and had decided to visit the gang himself. Ciccillo took to Salvatore at once. His innocent face, his evident honesty, his knowledge of the Neapolitan underworld, his fund of humorous stories, and his impartiality, made him the ideal link between the gang and the priests at the old church of the Materdei.

MEETING DON VESUVIO

CHARACTERS: *Salvatore*
Ciccillo
Members of the gang
Mario

SCENE 1: An Alley. The members of Ciccillo's gang are once again clustered around the fire.

1. Salvatore is telling Ciccillo and his friends about the old church, which he refers to as Don Vesuvio's place. (Mario is often called Don Vesuvio because of his quick temper—he flares up like Vesuvius, the volcano). Salvatore tells them of the advantages of living at the old church; there is plenty of food, decent beds, and honest work.

2. Mario enters. He is amazed to find Salvatore there, and getting on so well with Ciccillo. Ciccillo asks Salvatore

how he can meet this Don Vesuvio, and Salvatore points
to Mario. He tells them that Mario knows Don Vesuvio and
he can arrange a meeting between the two of them for the
following evening. Mario agrees.

3. Before leaving, Salvatore asks the group if he can take a
photograph of them, including Mario in the picture. They
agree. Salvatore and Mario go home.

SCENE 2: The following evening. Ciccillo's hideout. The
gang are again crouched around their fire.

1. Salvatore brings in Mario dressed as a priest. He is intro-
duced as Don Vesuvio. Ciccillo does not recognize him.

2. Mario, or Don Vesuvio, tells them that he would welcome
them at his old church, and they all agree to go with him.

3. Salvatore then shows them the photograph that he took
the previous evening. They point each other out with obvious
delight. Suddenly, Ciccillo spots Mario on the picture. He looks
at Don Vesuvio and back at the photograph again. He realizes
that Don Vesuvio is one and the same as the scugnizzo he
attacked two nights before. Full of shame at the way in which
he has treated Mario, and overwhelmed with gratitude for
what he is trying to do for them, Ciccillo seizes Mario by the
hand. 'It's you, Father', he blurts out. The strange lad who
never stole, never cheated, treated everyone with kindness
and consideration, and disappeared during the day, was not a
scugnizzo at all, but a Roman Catholic priest. Someone who
really cared for them, cared enough to become one of them
and share their poverty; cared enough now to be offering
them a home of their own where they could work and gain a
dignity they had never known before. The rest of the gang

crowd around Mario, hugging him, shaking his hand, patting him on the back. Although they would never have admitted it, what they were really seeking, more than anything else in the world, was love, and at last they had found a father with love enough for all of them.

4. Mario leads Ciccillo and his gang towards the old church of the Materdei like a modern Pied Piper.

Mario spent a total of 7 months as a scugnizzo, his work virtually unknown to the outside world. And then Morris West, an Australian novelist, arrived in Naples. He had heard of Mario's work among the scugnizzi and felt that it had all the makings of a first class biography. He wrote the book *Children of the Sun* and it became an instant best-seller. Money began to pour in from sympathizers all over the world who wanted to give what they could to help the scugnizzi.

But Mario realized that it was not enough to help the scugnizzi, there should be no scugnizzi needing help in the first place. It is in the *barrache*, the appalling shanty town where 20,000 people eke out a miserable existence in indescribable poverty and degradation, where conditions are so bad that the authorities have had to erect a wall around it in order to hide its shame from the gaze of the foreign tourists, that the scugnizzi are born, among the broken homes and impoverished families.

Children are forced out into the world so that their parents can afford to bring up their younger brothers and sisters. Only 20·8% of the population have regular work, over 50% of these are boys under the age of 15 and they work a 15 hour day, 7 days a week, for a mere 1000 lire—about 13s. 4d. The scugnizzi problem must be stamped out here, at its very roots, decided Mario.

He moved into one of the shanties to be on the spot to rescue the boys when they leave home, and save them from a life on the streets by sending them to the old church or the *Casa dello Scugnizzi* (the House of the Urchins) as it is now called. Mario works in close contact with the parents and arranges for the boys to return home to visit their families each Sunday. Helpers came to join him, and in 1964 they were instrumental in forcing the authorities to rehouse 700 of the shanty town families in council flats by threatening to hold a public fast in the centre of Naples if better housing conditions were not made available.

Mario spent the night in the *barrache* and returned to the running of the House of the Urchins during the day. As the ranks of the reclaimed scugnizzi grew, Mario sought additional accommodation for his expanding family. He leased two unused wings of the Oratory, a religious house on the Via Duomo, and the older boys moved there to learn a trade, and eventually go out to work, leaving the younger scugnizzi behind at the House of the Urchins.

Mario had plans for a £500,000 children's village at Posillipo, situated on a headland overlooking the Bay of Naples, where all the scugnizzi, both young and old, could be together again, but it was not to be. He could not obtain planning permission, and the authorities would not re-classify the farmland, upon which the site was situated, as building land.

Instead, in 1967 the old church was pulled down and the young boys were moved to the Oratory while a new 4-storied House of the Urchins, with offices, living rooms, dormitories, showers, a laundry, kitchen, storage rooms, central heating, and a small lift, grew out of the ruins of the old site. Additional buildings were put up on the adjoining land, the whole covering an area of roughly 6000 square yards.

Mario now lives permanently in the *barrache*, leaving the running of the Casa to Don Spada's brother. When Mario has seen all the families moved out from the shanty town he intends to turn his attention to the re-housing of all the families in that other great spawning ground of the scugnizzi, the *Bassi*, the slums, where 34% of the Naples population still live in conditions almost as bad as those in the *barrache*.

Mario has reclaimed over a thousand scugnizzi, but there are still three to four thousand still roaming the streets. It costs £175 to feed, clothe and educate one scugnizzo for a year. Mario has to rely upon voluntary contributions and the sale of scrap iron. The Government gives him no financial assistance whatsoever.

If you would like to help Mario in this important work, donations may be sent to the address given on page 15. If you write to this address sending a large stamped addressed envelope you will receive a copy of the *Casa Dello Scugnizzi Newsletter* which will give you the latest information about Father Borrelli and his work among the Spinning Tops of Naples.

3. ABBÉ PIERRE
AND THE EMMAUS COMMUNITY OF
RAG PICKERS

The World is judged by its poverty.
ABBÉ PIERRE

Thou shalt love the Lord thy God with all thy heart, and with all thy soul, and with all thy mind. This is the first and great commandment. And the second is like unto it, Thou shalt love thy neighbour as thyself. On these two commandments hang all the law and the prophets.

ST. MATTHEW **22**.37–40

PRELIMINARY WORK

1. Try to find out as much as you can about the conditions in Paris at the end of the Second World War.

2. Try to get the following books for your school library. They each contain information about the Abbé Pierre and his work.

ABBÉ PIERRE *Abbé Pierre Speaks*. Speeches collected by L. C. Repland and translated by Cecily Hastings and George Lamb (Sheed and Ward, London).

SIMON Boris *Abbé Pierre and the Ragpickers* (Harvill). This is a biography of the Abbé Pierre.

(Various Authors) *Heroes of Our Time* (Gollancz).

IMPROVISATION

Imagine a tramp walking down a darkened city street. His ancient felt hat is stained with wear, his brown overcoat reaches almost to his ankles, his patched threadbare trousers hang above his ankles revealing the large holes in his shabby socks and the cracked white surfaces of his unpolished boots; a red scarf around his neck conceals his torn, unwashed shirt. His sole possession apart from the clothes he stands up in is his stout gnarled stick cut from a holly bush. Thirty years of sleeping out in the open in all weathers have crippled his legs with rheumatics and a stick is a useful support.

He climbs the steps of a Salvation Army Hostel, opens the door and pushes his way inside. 'Got a doss for the night, Guv?' he asks the attendant at the desk. . . .

As you consider this man, try to image the circumstances that caused him to leave his home, perhaps a wife, possibly a family, and become a tramp. Perhaps he once had money and an easy life, but heavy drinking and light-fingered friends quickly reduced him to poverty. Or, he may have had good prospects and an assured future before a German bullet in 1916 disorganized his life and embittered him against society.

Now in your groups improvise a scene showing one incident that could have contributed to his downfall.

THE ABBÉ PIERRE

Henri Grouès was born in the French city of Lyons in 1912. His father was a wealthy silk manufacturer who belonged to a Roman Catholic organization whose members devoted part of every Sunday to feeding and caring for about 40 down-and-outs from the poorest quarter of the town.

When Henri was 12 years old he went for the first time to the presbytery where the organization had its headquarters. He watched fascinated as his father shaved a tramp. Meeting these people soon made him realize that although they were wretched and unclean they were nevertheless entitled to kindness and consideration. He joined the organization and did what he could to help.

At 19 he decided to dedicate his life to the poor. He gave away all his money and possessions to hospitals and other charitable institutions, and became a Capuchin monk. After 7 years with the Capuchins he took up an appointment as an assistant priest in the town of Grenoble.

The Second World War broke out and France was invaded by the Germany Army. These were terrible days. Many Frenchmen were hounded and persecuted, but none more so than the Jews. In 1942 a party of Jews came to Henri's door seeking refuge from the Germans. Henri hid them willingly. News of his hospitality quickly spread and he was soon inundated with refugees fleeing from the Nazi regime.

He became an expert forger, and many Jews and French Resistance workers were able to slip across the border into neutral Switzerland because they carried false identity cards, birth certificates and military papers, all forged by Henri. He made out his thousandth false identity card for himself and on it he entered the fictitious name of Abbé Pierre, a name by which he has been known ever since.

He was a member of the *Maquis*—the French underground movement—and became their chaplain. Twice he was captured by the Germans, but each time managed to escape.

After the liberation he was decorated with the Legion of Honour, the Medal of the Resistance, and the Croix de Guerre. He went into politics and became a Deputy, a French Member of Parliament.

In need of a centre for his political activities and a home for the family of a friend, he rented a detached house with an acre of land on the outskirts of Paris for £50 a year. The house had stood empty for 2 years and was in a very dilapidated condition. The ground floor ceiling was in danger of collapse, there was no gas or electricity, the water pipes had burst and the drains were fractured. Pierre set to work on the repairs in his spare time. He called the house Emmaus after the small village outside Jerusalem where Christ had first appeared to his disciples and given them hope after his crucifixion.

At weekends Pierre let off parts of Emmaus to different organizations, choral groups and student societies, many of whom brought bedding and stayed overnight either in the house or in tents in the grounds.

The war had left France impoverished: vast numbers of

people had lost their homes, many were hungry, large areas of farmland had been churned up by the warring armies, and the livestock had been commandeered to feed the troops. French men and women, who had been deported to work in Germany, and those who had been released from prisoner of war camps, now returned to France, swelling the ranks of the homeless. Many found themselves unable to adjust to the post-war conditions and turned to crime as the only way of making a living.

The Government authorized very little building at this time, and large numbers of the homeless slept out of doors, huddled in gutters or over the hot air gratings in winter temperatures of 10 degrees below zero.

Pierre had no intention of providing a place for refugees when he first bought the house, but his generosity, friendship and help soon became known to the down-and-outs and the homeless, and one by one they turned up at his door.

One of the first to arrive was Etienne. Two years before he had been convicted for stealing a bicycle and the court had sent him to a reform school. Discipline was strict and sometimes unfair.

ETIENNE'S STORY

SCENE 1: The changing rooms at the Reform School.

CHARACTERS: *A Reform School Teacher*
Gaston—the school bully
Jacques—a sickly boy
Etienne
The Governor
Boys of the School

1. A group of the boys are changing back into their prison clothes after a football match. They talk about the game. The Teacher tells them to be ready by the time he gets back. He is going to get a spare football left out on the field.

2. Gaston, the bully, had been sent off the field by the Teacher for continually fouling the other players. Now that the Teacher has gone he dares any of the other players to accuse him of unfair play. Jacques, a sickly boy, who was excused from the match, but saw the game from the touchline, is the only one brave enough to stand up to Gaston. He accuses him openly of several deliberate fouls.

3. Gaston is furious with Jacques and turns on him savagely, punching him about the face and body. Jacques is no match for Gaston and he offers little resistance. The other boys crowd round supporting Gaston.

4. Etienne comes in. He has been doing some work for the Governor and missed the match. Seeing what is happening, he pulls Gaston away from Jacques. Gaston turns on Etienne. They fight.

5. The Teacher returns with the spare football. The boys slink back to their lockers. Finding Gaston and Etienne fighting, the Teacher tells them to report to the Governor's office in the morning.

SCENE 2: The Governor's Office

CHARACTERS: *Gaston*
                Etienne
                The Governor

The Governor questions the boys to find out why they were fighting. Gaston accuses Etienne of starting the fight. Etienne tries to explain what really happened. The Governor has heard enough. He tells them to be quiet, and sentences them to three days solitary on bread and water.

Three days later Etienne, embittered by the injustice of the Governor's sentence, decides to escape. . . .

SCENE 3: In your groups show how Etienne escapes from the Reform School. There are high walls around the School with barbed wire on top, and an alarm system. Others can escape with Etienne if you wish, but because of what happens later neither Etienne nor his friends must harm anyone in gaining their freedom.

Once free, Etienne wandered the streets of Paris, avoiding the police, sleeping rough, and trying to feed himself as best he could.

SCENE 4: An orchard in the grounds of a convent school.

CHARACTERS: *Etienne*
                A class of French girls
                A teacher

1. Etienne jumps down from a wall into the convent orchard. He picks up a windfall apple and eats it. He talks to himself: 'These apples taste good. Wonder what place this is? Looks like a school.'

2. A party of schoolgirls appear. Etienne hides behind a tree. The girls spot him and ask him who he is and what he is doing in their orchard.

3. Etienne is shy at first, but because they are so friendly he eventually tells them all his troubles.

4. The girls feel sorry for him and give him some food from

their baskets—they have just come from a Domestic Science lesson. Etienne eats the food hungrily.

5. One of the girls notices that a teacher is coming. They tell Etienne to climb back over the wall. Etienne climbs the wall and disappears.

6. The teacher wants to know what they have been doing in the orchard. (*Make up your own excuse.*) She sends them on their way.

Etienne found food difficult to come by, and it became very cold out of doors as winter drew on. At last, in desperation, he went to Emmaus. He told Pierre the whole story: the theft of the bicycle, the Reform School, his escape, and his life on the run.

Pierre realized that although Etienne had not served his full sentence he had more than made up for his crime in the hardships he had endured in his wanderings. Unsure what to do with him, Pierre contacted a friend of his, an influential judge. The judge suggested that Pierre keep Etienne at Emmaus. He would, of course, deny any knowledge of this, and the police search for Etienne would have to be continued, but, in view of the latest developments, he would recommend that the authorities continue their search for Etienne beyond the Paris boundaries.

Soon after Etienne's arrival, Louis the Kangaroo came to Emmaus. He was 43 and had been a highly successful professional boxer before the war. In the ring his action reminded people of a boxing kangaroo, hence the nickname. He became a soldier at the outbreak of the war, but was captured by the Germans. Unable to keep up the constant practice so necessary for a first-class boxer to keep in trim, he lost all his old skills, and the Kangaroo became an ox. When he returned to France at the end of the war he was looked upon as a has-been. He tramped from one boxing promoter to another seeking work.

LOUIS THE KANGAROO

SCENE 1: Bernstein's office at his private gymnasium.

CHARACTERS: *Francois Bernstein—a boxing promoter*
                Albert Lenoir—an up-and-coming boxer
                Louis the Kangaroo

1. Bernstein is seated at his desk talking to a young up-and-coming boxer, Albert Lenoir. He tells Lenoir that with his record there is a great future for him in the ring.

2. Louis knocks on the office door and Bernstein asks him to come in. Bernstein asks him what he wants. Louis proudly tells him of his boxing successes before the war. Bernstein vaguely remembers him, but explains that he is now too busy promoting his new boy to care much for older men.

3. Louis pleads with him to be allowed a fight, just one to show what he can do.

4. To give him a chance Bernstein suggests that he has a try-out with Lenoir.

SCENE 2: In the ring.

1. Louis and Lenoir are sparring, but it is obvious from the very beginning that Louis' days of glory are over. Lenoir continually puts him down on the canvas. Bernstein has to stop the fight.

2. Bernstein tells Louis that he has a job for him: he can sweep out the ring, look after the boxing equipment, and now and again help out with the training of new boxers. Louis agrees —he desperately needs work.

Louis begins to take drugs to keep in shape. . . .

SCENE 3: Bernstein's gymnasium.

CHARACTERS: *André Briand—a young boxer*
Louis
Bernstein
Other boxers

1. Louis is demonstrating his once successful footwork to André Briand, but he is feeling off colour and has to lean against the ropes to pull himself together. Briand is becoming annoyed with his incompetent trainer.

2. Bernstein walks in and asks Louis how André is shaping. André complains bitterly. He wants to learn to be a boxer. He has not come here to be wet-nurse to a down-and-out.

3. Louis takes a bottle of tablets out of his pocket, unscrews the lid, taps out two pills, and swallows them.

4. Bernstein asks him what he is doing. Louis tells him that they are pills that his doctor has recommended for his nerves.

5. To Bernstein drugs and sport do not mix. He is furious with Louis. A good boxer is created by constant training, not drugs.

6. Two other boxers come in. Bernstein calls them over and asks them to throw Louis out. 'I don't want to see him around here again. If he does, you know what to do!'

Louis is now out of work. He begins to drink heavily in a sportsman's café. He hopes that people will recognize him and remember the time when his name was a household word in boxing circles. But most of the time he has to do his own remembering.

SCENE 4: A sportsman's café.

CHARACTERS: *Man in the café*
                Louis
                The proprietor
                Two young boxers
                Other people in the café
                Gendarmes

1. A man is drinking at the bar. Louis walks over to him and begins to talk of the great days of boxing before the war when he was a champion. The man is bored. Louis has told the same story too many times already.

2. Two young boxers come in. Hearing Louis' tale for the umpteenth time, they decide to liven things up by teasing him. 'You're not much of a champion now, are you, Grandad?' 'Where's the Kangaroo?' 'Must have gone back to Australia.' (One imitates the action of a Kangaroo while the other cheers wildly.)

3. This is more than Louis can stand. Throwing self-control to the wind, he lashes out at the two men with all the pent-up fury he can muster. The proprietor rings for the police.

4. A number of gendarmes rush in, and Louis turns on them as they try to pin him down. He fights like a madman. This is his last fight and he wants to be remembered for it.

5. The police eventually overpower him and he is hustled outside.

In court Louis was sentenced to three months imprisonment. Broken in body and mind he finally turned up at Emmaus.

Pierre did not care where a person came from, where he had been, or what his religion was, if any. 'It is enough for me to know that you are a man', he told the increasing number of vagrants who came to Emmaus.

News of his hospitality spread like wildfire through the poorer quarters of Paris and soon Emmaus could take no more. Temporary buildings were put up in the grounds, and men like Louis and Etienne gained a new purpose in life, helping to build inexpensive flats for the homeless using bricks bought from demolition firms.

The buildings spilled out from Emmaus onto bombed sites and waste ground. Shanty towns began to spring up. When they ran out of bricks Pierre accommodated the homeless families in derelict buses and in a collection of huts that had been built by the Germans to house prisoners of war which Pierre bought and re-erected at Neuilly-Plaisance near Paris.

Very little official building was being done at this time, but the authorities became increasingly concerned about the effects that Pierre's haphazard building programme was having upon town planning. They were annoyed too that the Social Welfare Centres were being boycotted by the needy who preferred to seek help from Emmaus rather than the State. Pierre was visited by a series of officials. One told him that he had no permit to build and that his hygiene arrangements were entirely unsatisfactory; in fact, he was breaking the law. Pierre pointed to a nearby woman who was expecting a baby: 'She is living in a tent at the moment. What are you going to do about it?' The official hurried away.

Another official inspected one of Pierre's building sites and informed him that the official frontage of a building should be 9 metres—Pierre's was 22 metres. Pierre explained that the building started off as a house for two families, but while it was being built more families turned up, and, as he had materials left over, he had decided to extend the frontage of the building to accommodate the extra families. The official regretted the circumstances, but felt that neither he nor his Ministry could allow Pierre to carry on building in this way. Pierre promised that he would stop building if the official guaranteed to find more satisfactory accommodation for the homeless. The official left hurriedly and never bothered Pierre again.

Eventually the frontage of the house grew to 70 feet, it had 15 rooms, and gave shelter to five families. It was built in 4 months at a cost of £900. Pierre's only expense lay in the materials; the labour was provided free of charge by people like Etienne, Louis, and crowds of Youth Hostellers who came to Paris from many different countries to help Pierre in his work.

Pierre lost his seat in the General Election of 1951 and decided to take up his Emmaus work full-time. He also lost the salary that he was paid as a Member of Parliament; from now on he would have to finance his building projects solely from voluntary contributions and from people who rented rooms at Emmaus.

With little money coming in, Pierre could not keep up with the demand for housing that came from people like Michel and Yvette.

MICHEL AND YVETTE

SCENE 1: The small room that Michel and his wife have shared with seven other members of their family for the past 3 years.

CHARACTERS: *Michel's mother*
Yvette—Michel's wife
Michel

1. Michel's invalid mother is lying in a bed in the corner. Yvette is trying to cook a meal on an oil stove in another part of the room.

2. The old woman begins to nag Yvette: she is cold and wants Yvette to close the window. Yvette complains that it will be too stuffy, but she does as she is told.

3. The old woman complains that Daniel, Yvette's baby boy, sleeping peacefully in the other bed in the room, kept her awake during the night with his crying. Yvette explains that she was kept awake too. 'Well, he's your child', snaps the old woman. 'Yes, and you're his grandmother', returns Yvette.

4. The old woman grumbles that she is hungry. Yvette tells her to wait until dinner time. She tells Yvette that she cannot wait.

5. She demands a drink of water. Yvette tells her that she is too busy cooking the meal. If the room had a sink it would be different, but it is a long way to the nearest tap.

6. (*Carry on this scene yourselves with Michel's mother continually nagging and bullying Yvette until she can stand it no longer.*) Yvette begins to complain about her mother-in-law's nagging. A furious row develops.

7. Michel comes in from work and does his best to stop the argument, telling Yvette that the rest of the family will be back shortly wanting their dinner.

Michel and Yvette have little time together, but on this particular occasion Michel has left work early and his mother is asleep in bed.

SCENE 2: The same room.

CHARACTERS: *Michel*
             Yvette
             Michel's mother
             Mitchel's older sister

1. Yvette complains to Michel about having to share their one room with his mother and father, his divorced elder sister, and her little boy.

2. Michel points out that he has to put up with her fifteen-year-old sister and her nineteen-year-old brother.
(*Note: There are only the two beds in the room. Michel, Yvette, and Daniel sleep in one; Michel's father, mother, his older sister and her little boy sleep in the other; Yvette's brother and sister both sleep on the floor.*)

3. Yvette feels that all the arguing that goes on is bad for Daniel and she longs for a house of her own.

4. Michel tells her that he hasn't the money to rent a room elsewhere.

5. He asks her if she wants him to do the shopping. She tells him that he only wants to run the errands so that he can be out of the house as much as possible. She tells him the groceries that she needs. (*Make up your own list, Yvette.*) Michel goes out to do the shopping.

6. Michel's mother wakes up and accuses Yvette of talking about her behind her back. This is too much for Yvette. She is sick and tired of the old woman's nagging, her father-in-law's drinking, and the smell in the room because her mother-in-law does not wash, change her sheets or her bedclothes, and won't allow the windows to be opened. Yvette begins to yell and scream. At the height of her mental breakdown she smashes the window to let some fresh air into the room.

6. Michel comes back from shopping with his elder sister. He slaps Yvette's face. She calms down. He sends his sister for the doctor.

7. His mother, now that she has a chance to speak again, pours out a string of abuse against Yvette, telling Michel that he should never have married such a creature and that Yvette is fit only for a lunatic asylum.

Poor Yvette did go to an asylum. When she was better Michel went to Father Pierre and he allowed Yvette a room in one of his houses.

He thought Michel's story of the frustrations of over-crowding was an exceptional one, but he was wrong. The tragic story of Marcel and Germaine was even more scanda-lous.

MARCEL AND GERMAINE

(Marcel and Germaine began married life sharing a flat with Marcel's friend, Claude. And then one day. . . .)

SCENE 1: Claude's flat in Paris.

CHARACTERS: *Marcel*
Germaine—his wife
Claude—their friend

1. Marcel and Germaine are sitting on the settee in Claude's flat. Germaine tells Marcel how lucky they are to be able to share this flat with Claude when many other people like themselves are homeless.

2. Claude comes home from work. Something seems to be troubling him. He talks about the weather and his work;

but he cannot keep the truth from them for very long. He tells them that he is getting married and he needs the flat for himself and his future wife. Marcel and Germaine will have to leave.

3. They congratulate Claude on his good news and tell him that they will soon find a flat of their own.

Marcel does manage to rent a flat. Germaine has a baby.

SCENE 2: Marcel's flat.

CHARACTERS: *Germaine*
Mrs. Dupoyt—the landlady
Marie Dupoyt—her daughter

1. Germaine is talking to her 18-month-old baby, telling her that they must go out to buy some milk. She leaves the flat taking the baby with her.

2. The landlady lets herself into Germaine's flat with a master key, her daughter comes with her. The landlady complains about Marcel, Germaine and the baby. (*Make up your own list of complaints, landlady.*) She tells her daughter that she has had enough: the woman, her husband and baby must go. Together they throw out all Germaine's belongings. The landlady keeps Germaine's coat.

3. Germaine returns with the baby to find all her possessions out in the corridor. The landlady orders her to leave and tells her that if she wants her coat back she must pay the rent up to date.

They manage to find a room in a cheap hotel.

SCENE 3: A bedroom in a small Parisian hotel. It is night time.

CHARACTERS: *First woman*
             Second woman
             The Hotel Manager
             A maid
             Marcel
             Germaine

Two women are trying to get some sleep, but they are continually being disturbed by the sound of a baby crying in the next room. They agree to see the Manager and register a complaint in the morning.

SCENE 4: The Manager's office, the next morning.

1. The Manager is sitting at his desk. The two women walk in and ask if they can have a word with him. They complain that the baby, crying in the next room, kept them awake all night. They tell him that either the family with the baby are moved or they will find alternative accommodation.

2. The Manager calls one of the maids and asks her to send him the couple from room number 4.

3. Marcel and Germaine walk into the office. The Manager tells them of the women's complaint and asks them to take the baby elsewhere.

SCENE 5: A café in Paris.

(*Marcel has sent Germaine and the baby to a Salvation Army Hostel while he stays on at the hotel. They meet for a short time each evening in a café.*)

CHARACTERS: *Germaine*
             Waitress
             Marcel

1. Germaine comes into the café and orders a cup of coffee from the waitress.

2. Marcel joins Germaine at her table. She tells him that she is fed up with living in a Salvation Army Hostel. He tells her that he is tired of being separated from her and living in the hotel.

3. Germaine tells Marcel that people have suggested that she put the baby into a home and ask for her back when they have found a place for themselves.

4. Marcel decides that they will be together. If no one will give them a room, then they must live out of doors. He knows a place on the quay, by the river. They will live there.

But living out of doors was far from satisfactory, especially with a young baby. Marcel goes to the Town Hall to see what can be done about getting accommodation.

SCENE 6: The Town Hall housing department.

CHARACTERS: *Town Hall official*
Marcel

1. Marcel walks up to the official seated behind the counter and tells him he has nowhere for his wife and child to live. They are having to sleep out in the open. He has had to leave a flat because his friend was getting married. They have been thrown out of a hotel because the baby's crying disturbed the other guests. They are now living out in the open. They cannot even light a fire because the police will spot them and sleeping out in the open is against the law.

2. The clerk takes his name and tells him that he will put him on the priority list, but explains that there are 64,000 applicants already and only 900 cheap flats available.

3. Marcel thanks him and walks away. The situation is hopeless.

They moved away from the quay and sought shelter under a bush protected by a fence at the bottom of a railway embankment. They slept in their clothes, wrapped up in a blanket. The baby slept in its pram. They dared not light a fire for fear of attracting attention—vagrancy was forbidden by law. Learning of their plight, Claude lent them a tarpaulin which Marcel draped over a simple framework to make a tent. But the tarpaulin leaked, and when it rained water dripped onto the pile of straw which served as their bed. The winter rains soon transformed their surroundings into a quagmire. Germaine had another baby which she kept in a crib made out of a soap box. It was very cold.

SCENE 7: Inside Marcel's tent.

CHARACTERS: *Marcel*
                Germaine
                The doctor

1. Germaine is trying to cook a meal on their cheap stove. Marcel comes home from work. Germaine grumbles about the appalling conditions under which they live. She asks Marcel why he does not try to build his own house. He explains that they would need at least £100 deposit just to buy a site and have the water and electricity laid on. They will be a long time saving that kind of money out of the £4 a week he brings home in wages.

2. Germaine goes to look at the baby. Something seems to be wrong with it. She sends Marcel out to get a doctor.

3. The doctor arrives. He tells them that the baby has pneumonia. It must be moved to hospital at once.

SCENE 8: At the hospital.

CHARACTERS: *Marcel*
                Germaine
                The Matron of the hospital.

1. The matron is sitting at her desk filling in a form. Marcel and Germaine go up to her and ask how the baby is. She tells them that it died during the night. Germaine breaks down. She blames Marcel. A furious row develops between them. The Matron steps in and tries to calm them both.

Marcel and Germaine could not afford to give the baby a decent burial—it was interred in a common grave. Marcel began drinking heavily to forget his sorrows.

SCENE 9: A bar in Paris.

CHARACTERS: *Marcel*
                A barman
                Customers

1. Marcel is drinking at the bar. He has had too much to drink already. He tells the barman and the customers his sorry tale. (*Tell it in your own words, Marcel.*)

2. The customers either sympathize with him or find him a bore. The barman tells him that he has had enough to drink. Marcel demands a further drink, but the barman refuses to serve him.

3. The barman asks some of the customers to give him a hand to carry Marcel outside.

Meanwhile Pierre discovered Germaine carrying 2 pails of water. Pierre offered to carry her pails home for her.

When he discovered where she lived he immediately offered her a room in one of his houses.

15,000 people were living in hotels and many others were paying out more than half their wages for just one room with no facilities for either washing or preparing meals. Altogether 7,000,000 men, women and children all over France were suffering from the housing shortage caused by the war. There was much selfishness: the owners of many of the larger houses could easily have let off their unused servant's quarters and spare rooms to the homeless but few did. Many were later to say, 'If only we had known'. Hospitals, prisons and poor houses were full to overflowing, and the law courts were constantly in session sentencing those who, in desperation, had turned to crime in order to live.

Defying the authorities' ban, Pierre began to develop another site at Champs Fleuris. He realized that once he could get the houses built and people living in them the authorities would find it difficult to evict them, because if they did they would have to find them alternative accommodation, which Pierre knew was virtually impossible. Pierre and his amateur builders worked in shifts around the clock in order to move in as many families as possible before the authorities became aware of what was happening.

It was not long before Champs Fleuris had a visit from an official from the Ministry of Housing who told Pierre that his shanty towns had been put up without Government permission and were therefore illegal. This annoyed Pierre intensely. He accused the official and his Department of negligence in not providing adequate housing after the war. He threatened him that if he was pestered again by the housing authorities he would notify the press and television of the appalling conditions under which Marcel and Germaine, Michel and Yvette had been living before he rescued them and placed them in his so-called illegal homes, which official-dom was now threatening to close. The official decided that perhaps his Department would not prosecute after all. He would see what he could do. He left hurriedly.

He returned a year later with the news that Pierre could finish the buildings that he had already begun, but he must not build any new ones of the same type.

19 houses were finished at Champs Fleuris and Pierre moved on to a second site at Les Coquelicots where he erected 14 more illegal homes.

In the meantime Pierre was desperately short of money and his debts began to accumulate. He was forced to sell his car.

A CROIX DE GUERRE GOES BEGGING

(*In your groups draft out a letter explaining why the Abbé Pierre is having to build cheap houses, include something about the people who will live in them, and end the letter by asking for money to enable Pierre to carry on with his work. During these trying times some people thought nothing of spending 10,000 francs (roughly £10) on a meal.*)

CHARACTERS: *A party of diners*
A waiter
The Abbé Pierre

SCENE: The Rivoli Restaurant, Paris.

1. A group of people are sitting at one of the dining tables, each reading through a copy of the menu. They are deter-mined to enjoy themselves at all costs. The waiter walks over

to their table and asks if he can take their order. One of the party begins to order:

Soupe Oignon	Onion Soup
Coté de Veau	Veal
Petit Pois	Peas
Pommes de Terre Sautés	Potatoes
Ananas à la Crème	Pineapples and Cream
Fromage Camembert	Cheese

(*Choose your own meal, diner, if you would rather, but let it be something special.*)

2. The Abbé Pierre walks into the restaurant, wearing his decorations. He walks across to the diners and hands them a copy of his letter. (*It is the one that you have just written in your groups.*)

3. One of the diners reads the letter to the rest. Pierre begs for money in order to continue his building projects.

4. Finish off the scene for yourselves. How many of you feel guilty and drop a few francs into his tin? Bear in mind that in a whole evening's begging around some of the most expensive restaurants in Paris Pierre only collected 2000 francs (about £2—just enough to feed his vagrants for a couple of days). How many of you refuse to give Pierre anything at all? Give him your reasons. (*Note: You dare not send for the Manager to have him thrown out, as Pierre is wearing his medals—the highest honours that France can bestow.*)

5. End your scene with Pierre leaving the restaurant.

One evening after dinner back at Emmaus, Pierre tells his friends that he has some bad news for them.

THERE'S MONEY IN OTHER PEOPLE'S RUBBISH

CHARACTERS: *The Abbé Pierre*
Philippe—a rag-picker
A group of Pierre's needy friends

SCENE: The dining room at Emmaus.

1. Pierre announces that they have no more money. They must all eat less or find somewhere else to go.

2. Philippe asks if he can make a suggestion. He is a rag-picker who spends his time fishing in dust bins for bones, paper and junk, which he sells to pulp merchants and dealers. He can earn 500 francs (about 10/-) a day doing this.

3. He tells them that before the war a well-known rag-picker organized his friends into a syndicate and became a millionaire within 3 years. Many people are taking it up as a way of making money. Whole families are employed collecting the stuff, sorting it, patching it up and selling it again, making enough money in the winter to be able to spend the summer driving around Cannes and Monte Carlo in the latest American cars.

4. Another way of making money, suggests Philippe, is to wheel a hand-cart from house to house and sell the items collected on the flea markets at Port St. Ouen or in the Rue Mouffetard on Sunday mornings. People are making £1000 a year doing this.

5. Pierre asks his friends for their opinions. They agree to take up rag-picking themselves.

But rag-picking is not as easy as it seems. . . .

YOU LEAVE MY RAGS ALONE!

CHARACTERS: *A group of Pierre's friends turned rag-pickers*
             A professional rag-picker
             The driver of a dust-cart

SCENE: A row of dustbins in a Parisian alleyway.

1. Pierre's friends are sorting out the marketable items from the rest of the garbage. (*What do they find? Tell your friends.*)

2. One of them cuts his hand on a piece of broken glass. He is worried in case he will get tetanus.

3. A professional rag-picker arrives. He asks to see their police permit entitling them to search dustbins. They confess that they do not have permits. He tells them that they are trespassing on his patch and threatens them with violence if they do not leave his dustbins alone.

4. The driver of a dust-cart appears and asks the cause of the dispute. The rag-picker explains the situation: Pierre's men introduce themselves.

5. Hearing that they are from Emmaus, the driver of the dust-cart is immediately on their side. His mother once lived in one of Pierre's houses and since that time he has had nothing but praise for the Abbé's work.

6. He tells Pierre's friends that they can carry on with their rag-picking. There are more bins down the alleyway for the professional rag-picker to pick over.

7. The professional rag-picker storms off down the alley muttering to himself.

When Pierre learns of this incident he realizes that they must not break the law again, they must concentrate upon house-to-house collections in future. Before sending his men from door to door he made sure that each householder to be visited received a letter explaining that his friends would be collecting old rags, clothes, scrap metal, junk of any sort, to sell to help the poor. People responded eagerly. Attics were ransacked for stuffed birds, lamps, musical instruments; clothes that had been hoarded for years were parcelled up, and books bundled together, ready to be collected by Pierre's helpers. Everything was sold to a wholesale dealer.

They rarely came home empty-handed, but on one occasion Pierre received a telephone call from a woman living on the other side of Paris who told him that if his people called at her flat they would receive something worthwhile. Pierre sent three of his assistants with a handcart across Paris in the middle of a blinding hailstorm.

AND YOU'VE BROUGHT US ALL THIS WAY— FOR THAT!

CHARACTERS: *Gaspare*
Chicot } *Pierre's helpers*
Auguste
Bertha—Madame Reyner's maid
Madame Reyner

SCENE: Outside Madame Reyner's flat.

1. Gaspare, Chicot, and Auguste stop outside Madame Reyner's flat. Gaspare looks at the piece of paper that Pierre has given him with the address on. He confirms that this is the correct address: Number 16 Concorde Mansions. Auguste rings the bell.

2. Bertha answers the door. They introduce themselves and ask to see Madame Reyner. Bertha goes off leaving them on the doorstep. They discuss the various things that this worthwhile object might be: a wardrobe? A settee? (*Make up your own list.*) The maid keeps them waiting a long time.

3. At last Madame Reyner appears and apologizes for keeping them waiting. She asks them if they are hungry. Expecting a meal they tell her that they are.

4. She ignores this and asks them about the Abbé Pierre and his work. (*Make up your own questions, Madame Reyner.*) She tells them that she has heard many interesting things about Emmaus and feels that no words can express the vital work that they are all doing for the homeless.

5. She asks each of them in turn to explain how they came to be working with Pierre. (*Make up your own stories Gaspare, Chicot and Auguste.*)

6. At long last she tells them that she will fetch the article. Once again they are left standing on the doorstep. After another long wait she comes back, thrusts an object into Gaspare's hands, wishes them luck and closes the door in their faces. Gaspare unwraps the parcel. Inside is a chipped fruit dish. They walk away down the corridor feeling very annoyed. 'She didn't even offer us a cup of coffee. I've a good mind to heave the blooming thing right back through her window', mutters Chicot.

To supplement the money brought in from the house collections Pierre decides to try some more rag-picking, this time on the dump where the dust-carts tip their rubbish. He obtains permission from the man in charge of the dump and 6 volunteers are sent, with a tent, to camp out there and work the tip full-time.

WE'VE ALL SUFFERED SOMETHING

CHARACTERS: *Brett*
             Lyle
             Guy
             Jacques   } *Pierre's 6 volunteers*
             Jean
             Henri
             The foreman
             Fernandel
             The Abbé Pierre

SCENE: The refuse tip.

1. The 6 volunteers are picking over the parts of the tip assigned to them by the foreman, but they can find nothing of value. The professional rag-pickers have been there before them. (*What do you find? Banana skins? A bundle of stained postcards? A book with pages 6–30 missing? A broken watch strap? Make up your own list of worthless items.*)

2. They ask the foreman if they can pick over the rubbish that has just been unloaded from the dust-carts. He agrees.

3. This annoys Fernandel, a professional rag-picker who lives in a caravan at the dump. He has first choice over all the new rubbish brought to the tip. He orders them to leave.

4. Remembering that the mention of Pierre's name earned their friends the support of a dust-cart driver the last time an argument broke out with a professional rag-picker, they proudly tell Fernandel that they work for the Abbé Pierre.

5. 'Haven't priests enough rubbish in their churches without taking mine?' retorts Fernandel.

6. Pierre joins them. He has come to see how they are getting on. They tell Pierre that Fernandel will not let them work the best part of the tip.

7. Fernandel's shirt is wide open. He has a tattoo of Christ's head on his chest. Underneath are written the words 'He has suffered', and over the crown of thorns the tattooist has inscribed 'So have I'.

Pierre. What a marvellous tattoo! When did you have that done?

Fernandel. In prison.

Pierre. We're going to get on fine.

Fernandel. That's O.K. by me.

8. Fernandel tells them that there is enough rubbish on the tip for all of them. They all begin rag-picking together.

And so Pierre divided his men into two groups: the rag-pickers and the builders. The rag-pickers earned the money so that the builders could carry on with their work. New building sites were being developed all the time, but there were never enough homes for the people in need of them—never enough money. All the rubbish had to be carried away by hand, and journey after journey was needed to collect enough junk to be worth selling. The rag-pickers with vans had all the advantages over Pierre's helpers with their little hand-carts. More money was desperately needed.

One evening, at a friend's house, Pierre listened to a recording of the radio quiz game 'Double or Quits'. It was compered by the famous French radio star Zappy Max, and sponsored by a well-known soap firm. Starting with 250 francs for the first correct answer, the contestants doubled their prize money for each correct answer given. Learning that the show was shortly to be broadcast from a circus tent pitched on the Chantilly road close to Paris, Pierre decided to become one of the contestants. Here was another way of raising money to help the poor.

He chose to answer questions on Current Affairs.

DOUBLE OR QUITS

CHARACTERS: *Zappy Max*
                His assistant
                The Abbé Pierre
                Members of the studio audience

SCENE: The Double or Quits circus tent on the Chantilly road.

(*Note: You can make up your own list of questions on French current affairs if you wish.*)

1. Zappy Max asks the next contestant to play Double or Quits. Pierre introduces himself and asks for questions on current affairs. He answers each question correctly.

2. The first question is: What is the population of France?
    (*Answer:* 46 million.)   250 francs (about 5/3d.).
    (*After each correct answer Zappy Max's assistant calls out the sum of money that Pierre has won and takes the notes out of a cash register.*)
    (b) What is the President's term of office?
    (*Answer:* 7 years.)   500 francs (10/6d.).
    (c) How far is it from Paris to Marseilles?
    (*Answer:* 761 kilometres.)   1000 francs (£1).
    (d) What is the date of the national pilgrimage to Lourdes?
    (*Answer:* 15th August.)   2000 francs (£2).

(e)   Name two books written by André Gide.
  (*Answer:* The Pastoral Symphony,
           The Narrow Door.)   4000 francs (c. £4).
  (f)   What percentage of the national expenditure goes on
defence?
  (*Answer:* 38%.)   8000 francs (£8).
  (g) How many M.P.s are there in the French Government?
  (*Answer:* 627.)   16,000 francs (£16).
  (Pierre had once been an M.P. himself.)
  (h) What is the parish church of the Latin Quarter of
Paris?
  (*Answer:* The Church of St.
           Severin.)   32,000 francs (£32).
  (i)   What do the initials F.A.O. stand for?
  (*Answer:* United Nations
           Food and Agricul-
           tural Organization.   64,000 francs (£64).
  (Pierre knew the man who had founded the Organiza-
tion.)
  (j)   How many Gold Medals did France win in the
Helsinki Games?
  (*Answer:* 6.)   128,000 francs (£128).
  (k) Who is the older: Churchill or Stalin?
  (*Answer:* Churchill.)   260,000 francs (£260).

3. Zappy Max asks Pierre if he wants to go on, but Pierre
decides to stop at 260,000 francs.

4. He asks Zappy Max if he can put a question to all the
people sitting in their homes listening to the broadcast. Zappy
Max agrees.

5. Pierre tells the radio audience of his work among the
homeless and asks for financial assistance to carry on with his
building projects.

The 260,000 francs was soon spent, but there was no end to the homeless families that came to Emmaus.

During the night of January 3rd–4th 1954, the temperature dropped to —10 degrees centigrade. At Pierre's building site at Les Coquelicots work was temporarily at a standstill, and one homeless family, with their 3-month-old baby sought refuge from the cold in an abandoned car beside the foundations of their future home. The baby, unable to stand the extreme conditions, died during the night.

At the same time the Council of the French Government rejected an Emergency Housing Plan put forward by Pierre and his friends which recommended a government-sponsored crash programme of inexpensive but durable tenements, that could be rented cheaply to the homeless. The Council viewed the housing crisis as a temporary affair, and envisaged a property boom by 1957, by which time Pierre's recommended tenements would be superfluous. They saw no point in financing houses which were shortly to become obsolete.

Pierre invited the Minister of Reconstruction to attend the baby's funeral. The Minister, surrounded by homeless families, followed the funeral procession on its mile-long journey. For the first time he saw France's poverty, not as a bundle of statistics on his desk, but at a personal level. After the funeral, Pierre took the Minister on a tour of his shanty towns. The Minister confessed that he had never seen such poverty before.

He realized the desperate need that there was for housing, and at the next meeting of the Council the Temporary Housing Bill was passed.

But it takes time to build houses and, in the meantime, people were dying of cold on the Parisian streets. Pierre could not leave them to die. He organized a refreshment service which toured pavements near the Gare de Lyon and the Gare d'Austerlitz where the homeless tried to get some sleep hunched over the warm air ventilators, providing them with blankets, soup, bread and wine.

People who previously spent the night in sheds and derelict buildings were now driven out onto the streets by the increasing cold, pacing up and down the pavements in an endeavour to keep warm.

Pierre was invited to appear on television and he used the opportunity to broadcast an appeal for help for the homeless. He described in graphic detail how he came upon what he took to be a pile of rubbish lying on the pavement. It was only when he took a closer look that he saw that it was not rubbish, but two old men, both blind, dying under a pile of sacking. Stray dogs are treated with more respect than stray human beings, he told his viewers. They, at least, are rounded up and taken to the pound; but, here in France, there is no pound for stray human beings.

A property owner hearing Pierre's broadcast gave him a plot of land in the centre of Paris, and he persuaded another who dealt in war surplus goods, to provide a large tent. The tent was quickly erected on the vacant site, a ton of straw was scattered over the floor and heaters were brought in. The tent was thrown open to the homeless. But it was too small to cater for the many who had nowhere to go.

A Committee for Urgent Aid to the Homeless was formed and two centres were set up to bring in the vagrants from off the streets. Out of a total of 125 wanderers, the helpers made the shocking discovery that 80% were not the flotsam and jetsam of society, but decent upright citizens, who, through no fault of their own, were trapped in the pitiless circumstances of having no place to go home to for the night.

Pierre made another broadcast. He told of the discovery of a woman's body at 3 o'clock in the morning, eviction papers clutched in her stiff cold hands. She had been thrown out of her lodgings because she owed £8 in rent. She had wandered the streets until death released her from her hopeless misery. He told of the 2000 homeless, hungry, and ill-clad people who slept out in the streets each night. He explained that the buildings promised by the Government would take weeks to complete. Something had to be done immediately. The weather reports forecast a worsening of the already arctic conditions. Money, food, blankets and clothing were desperately needed so that emergency centres could be set up as soon as possible. He asked his audience to send whatever they could to the Hotel Rochester near the Champs Élysées where the generous proprietress had already put 12 of her rooms at his disposal for the homeless.

This appeal caused an avalanche. The conscience of the nation had been aroused. Within an hour the streets leading to the Hotel were crowded with people. Extra police had to be brought in to divert the traffic and keep the crowd moving as hundreds flocked into the Hotel and deposited their gifts in the foyer. Small children emptied their money boxes; one man left his coat and walked away into the freezing cold outside, another handed over a package containing £1000, and one poor old woman gave all that she had—her wedding ring. Day after day letters poured in containing cheques and money (£500,000 in all), while the subways, railway stations, private hotels and public buildings opened their doors to the outcasts.

Pierre began a crash building programme financed by the money sent to the Hotel and the homeless families began to move off the streets and out of their derelict buses into new homes, the whole process made possible by the tireless efforts of the Abbé Pierre and his small community of rag-pickers.

SHELTER

France is not the only country to have a housing problem. Today in Britain, in cities like London, Glasgow, Birmingham and Liverpool, 3 million families are living in overcrowded slum conditions, and 12,500 people are forced to live in hostels for the homeless because they can find no place of their own. 5000 children are separated from their parents and in the care of local authorities because of the pitiful circumstances in which their parents live.

These are just a few of the figures quoted by *Shelter, the National Campaign for the Homeless*. Relying upon voluntary subscriptions, *Shelter* aims to rehouse one homeless family a day—families in danger of splitting up because of the appalling conditions in which, through no fault of their own, they have to live. *Shelter* wants to badger the authorities to speed up their housing programmes, to assist voluntary housing associations in buying old houses and converting them into decent houses for families in desperate need of somewhere to live, and to publicize the urgent needs of the homeless.

It takes an average of £325 to rehouse one homeless family and already *Shelter* has collected more than £200,000 and rehoused a total of 1200 people.

If you would like to help *Shelter* in this vital work, donations may be sent to: Shelter, National Campaign for the Homeless, 86 The Strand, London W.C.2.

You can learn more about *Shelter* and their work for the British homeless by writing to the above address enclosing a large stamped addressed envelope.

4.   DANILO DOLCI

As you did it to one of the least of these my brethren, you did it to me.

ST. MATTHEW **25**.40

PRELIMINARY WORK

1. Draw a map of Sicily showing the following: Palermo, Partinico, Trappeto, Sciari, Balestrate, the River Iato, the Gulf of Castellamare, the Gulf of Selinunte, Sciacca, Roccamena, Corleone and Menfi.

2. What are the differences between Roman Catholics and Communists? What do each believe in?

3. Try to obtain the following books for your school library; they each contain information about Sicily, Danilo Dolci and the Mafia.

BARZINI Luigi *The Italians* (Hamish Hamilton).

DOLCI Danilo *To Feed the Hungry*.

DOLCI Danilo *The Outlaws of Partinico*.

DOLCI Danilo *Waste*.

DOLCI Danilo *For The Young*.

(These are Danilo's famous reports on the social conditions of Western Sicily published by MacGibbon and Kee.)

GUERCIO Francis M. *Sicily: Garden of the Mediterranean* (Faber).

LEWIS Norman *The Honoured Society* (Collins). (The blood-drenched story of the Mafia.)

MCNEISH James *The Fire Under the Ashes* (Hodder and Stoughton). (Danilo's official biography.)

MAXWELL Gavin *The Ten Pains of Death* (Longmans). (Another account of the social conditions of Western Sicily.)

(Various Authors) *Heroes of Our Time* (Gollancz).

4. The Danilo Dolci Trust publishes a News-Bulletin about Dolci and his work. You will receive the latest copy by writing to The Danilo Dolci Trust, 29 Great James Street, London W.C.1, enclosing a large stamped addressed envelope.

The Trust also hires out a film entitled *Murder by Neglect*. It is an account of the Sicilians and the conditions under which they live and shows how Dolci is attempting to improve these conditions. It was first shown on BBC Television. The hire charge is 10/6d. per booking.

5. Another film about Danilo Dolci called *Mafia No!* by David Naden Associates is a colour record of Dolci's March of Protest and is available for an inclusive hire charge of £3 from Concord Film Council, Nacton, Ipswich, Suffolk.

IMPROVISATION

Imagine that there is something that you desperately need, but your parents will not let you have it. It might be a dress, or a bicycle, or they may have refused you permission to go somewhere or to stay out late at night.

In your groups make up two scenes:

In Scene 1 you ask your father or mother for the thing that you want. They refuse and you tell them that you are going to go without food until they give in to your request? How do they react to this?

Scene 2 will show what happens the following day. The rest of your family are sitting around the table having their lunch. You are hungry and your parents are concerned about your hunger strike. Show how one of you gives in. Do you begin eating again? Or do your parents agree to your request?

SICILY

Sicily is the largest island in the Mediterranean, situated south-west of the 'toe' of Italy. Most of the land is over 1000 feet above sea level, and the rain, which falls mainly in the winter, strips off the soil as it plunges in torrents down to the Mediterranean Sea. The swollen streams often change course leaving behind a dried-up river bed littered with stones where once there had been fertile farmland. The age-old practice of ploughing down the hillsides rather than across them breaks up the soil even more, as the water rushes down the furrows turning them into gullies carrying away the fertile topsoil. The high landscape of the interior has become a barren desert; the parched and cracked earth is scored by deep crevices.

The land need not be infertile. With reservoirs and aqueducts the desert could be made to bloom again as it did in Roman times, but for the ingrained obstinacy of the people who believe that 'what was good enough for my father is good enough for me'. Progress on the island is frustrated by those who think that poverty is a judgement from God for the sins of the people, who place more faith in mumbo jumbo than in modern technology. A peasant was recently told by his priest that in order to prevent landslides on his property he must sprinkle his farm with the holy water from 7 churches. They consider that stable manure dirties the land, and instead of using it as a fertiliser, they collect it from the stables and pile it in heaps on the outskirts of towns, which become breeding grounds for flies and hazards to public health. Housewives often use these heaps as places to dump the hot ashes from their fires; these set the drying heaps ablaze and the fires can burn for several days, the wind blowing the acrid smoke through the towns and into the houses.

Few cows are kept, owing to the shortage of water and the lack of grass. Sheep and goats are the principal livestock. What few cows there are are fed on hay mixed with the leaves of the prickly pear bushes that flourish in the Sicilian hedgerows, and the milk that they give is far less nutritious than that from grass-fed cows.

The Feudal System, with its Lord of the Manor, its antiquated method of farming, and its restrictive laws, applied with great severity to the down-trodden serfs slaving on their meagre strips of land for the profit of their masters, is still very much a feature of the Sicilian way of life. The country is divided into large estates; the owners leave the running of these to others, while they enjoy the sumptuous elegance of their Parisian villas or Roman mansions. They have no desire to change a system that has profited themselves and their forefathers since Norman times. So long as law and order is kept on their vast estates they see no reason to change the *status quo*.

In the past the estates were controlled by stewards, whose orders were enforced by armed guards, who bullied the peasants unmercifully as they worked the land for their masters. The stewards settled all disputes, and when the estates were threatened they raised private armies to defend their master's territories. Today the estates are taken over by *gabellotti*— singular *gabellotto*—literally tax collectors, who buy the feudal rights to the estates from the owners on a series of short-term leases at public auctions. These men are always *Mafiosi* (i.e. members of the *Mafia*: see the next chapter). The gabellotti lease out the land to tenant farmers taking 50% of their crops as rent. The gabellotti leave most of the responsibility for the running of the estates to managers and their overseers while they retire and live off the proceeds from the downtrodden peasant farmers.

The tenant farmer finds it difficult to make ends meet. He lacks the money to buy enough seed or equipment. If he borrows from a money-lender, he is burdened by the extortionate rates of interest—sometimes as much as 32% of the original loan. Half of his profits go to the gabellotto, and he is expected to pay a land dowry, roughly 15 stone of corn for every $2\frac{1}{2}$ acres gathered. He also has to contribute to the annual feast of the local saint, provide funds for the nearby church and monastery, keep up the roads and pay his armed guards. There is little money left over to pay the men who work for him. He is usually so impoverished that he can only afford to put them to work on a day-to-day basis, offering them perhaps three days work one week and two the next. These labourers are fortunate if they can get 120 working days in any one year.

Over half the population are employed as day-labourers living at or below the subsistence level. Because of unemployment there is keen competition for the few jobs available, and this situation has given rise to the infamous labour marts.

THE LABOUR MART

CHARACTERS: *A crowd of Sicilian day-labourers*
Gino Zarrone—a bully
Francesca Virda
Don Tracona—a landowner

SCENE: The church steps in a Sicilian town during the grape harvest. It is 4 a.m. and a crowd of day-labourers are sitting on the steps waiting for the landowners to arrive and offer them work. Each man carries a knife for cutting off the fruit from the vines and a large basket to collect it in.

The first to arrive sit on the bottom steps. When the owners come it is a question of first come, first employed. Latecomers queue on the higher steps. The men below are continually shifting down to make room for them. Sometimes more than a hundred men sit waiting for work. Some are dozing, some playing cards, others are reading, or talking about the problems of unemployment.

1. Gino Zarrone arrives late—he has overslept. He tries to jump the queue by pushing in front of Francesca Virda. Francesca complains, Gino draws his knife. 'All right. Let's fight for last place', cries Gino. The others stop what they are doing to watch, ready to support their favourite. The combatants make a lunge at each other. Gino tears Francesca's sleeve.

2. At this moment Don Tracona, a landlord, walks in. The fight is forgotten in the excitement of being offered a job. A group of labourers cluster around him. 'Are you taking anybody on this morning, Don Tracona?' asks one of the men. Tracona shakes his head. He looks at them, his hands in his pockets.

'I did a good job for you last summer, Don Tracona, Don't you remember me?' cries another. 'No, I don't', mumbles Tracona.

Several men try to gain Tracona's attention. (*Make up your own questions and answers.*)

3. At last, Tracona tells them that he wants four strong men who will work hard. Those at the bottom of the steps push forward. Tracona nudges an old man aside: 'You're too old, grandad.'

He inspects the rest, feeling their muscles. Those chosen are pushed to one side.

4. When he has selected four likely candidates, he walks over to them.

'How much do you want?' he asks.

'Eight hundred lire' (roughly 9/4d.), replies one of the men.

'To much. I'll pay you 600 lire' (7/-d.).

'That's not enough', says the man who asked for 800.

'Take it or leave it', replies Tracona.

The man walks back to the steps. Perhaps another land-owner will be along later offering 800 lire.

Turning to the other three Tracona asks them if they agree to the 600 lire. They nod their heads.

'Right. I want someone to take his place for 600 lire.' Other men push forward. He feels their muscles, selects one, and goes off taking his four workers with him.

5. The rest take their places back on the steps, hoping that there will be other employers later on.

Imagine that you were the man who turned down the 600 lire offer. You wait all day for an employer to come along offering a higher wage, but with no success. That night you go home to your wife and 9 children. She has heard that you turned down the 600 lire. Show what happens when you get home. End the scene by promising your wife that you will go out collecting firewood which you can exchange for 2 pounds (weight) of bread at the local bakery.

Unemployment has caused many Sicilians to emigrate. Between 1951 and 1961, more than 10% of the population sought work elsewhere, and for some of the others who could not afford to emigrate, a life of banditry seemed the only desperate way to make a living. There are large areas on the western part of the island where 80% of the men have spent more than a year in prison.

Many of the unemployed have become street sellers, selling water, boiled cuttle-fish, sea urchins, tiny shrimps, worms, fish bait, or, if they are really desperate, snails, which they sell to people too poor to buy butcher's meat. Others carry parcels for wealthy shoppers, or sell contraband cigarettes, a crime which carries severe penalties if they are caught by the police. Many supplement their low wages by gleaning in the fields. But even this has its dangers.

MURDERED FOR A FEW EARS OF CORN

CHARACTERS: *Gaspare Vidari—a gleaner*
Mario Brecchi—a landowner
An armed guard
A party of gleaners

SCENE: A party of unemployed day-labourers, their wives and children, are gleaning the ears of corn left after the harvesting on Mario Brecchi's estate. They are not allowed to touch the sheaves that are standing tied up waiting to be carted away. They sing as they fill their sacks with corn.

1. A gun is fired. They look up and see the landowner and one of his armed guards. The owner tells them to 'clear off'. He tells them that he needs the ears of corn lying on the ground to fatten his cattle.

2. The gleaners ignore him and carry on picking up the ears of corn. The armed guard points his gun at Gaspare Vidari, pulls the trigger, and Gaspare falls dead.

3. There is a stunned silence. No one goes to Gaspare's aid. 'Now clear off!', shouts the landowner. He tells them that if anybody asks what happened they are to say that Gaspare was stealing corn from the sheaves, the guard caught him, there was a scuffle, and the guard fired in self-defence. They all agree to this, knowing full well that if they say otherwise they will never be allowed to work or glean again. The landowner orders them to empty their sacks before they leave.

4. They empty their sacks and walk sadly away. The owner orders his guard to remove Gaspare's body.

Sicily has always been a violent country. To protect themselves from attacks by outlaws, the landowners built their houses, administrative buildings, warehouses and granaries like giant fortresses situated far from the towns where the labourers live. Consequently the day-labourer spends a great deal of his time walking to and from work. Sometimes, when there is much to be done, the labourers are allowed to live on the estates in the straw shelters where the tools are kept. because of their short term of tenure, the tenant farmers and the gabellotti make no improvements to the property; it is handed over just as they found it, always in a state of decay.

In 1948 Sicily was granted a form of self-government controlled from Rome. Elections are held every four years and 90 Members of Parliament are sent to the Regional Assembly, which is the local Parliament. There are two main political parties: the Christian Democrats and the Communists. The Christian Democrats are supported by the Roman Catholic Church, and because the people are so deeply religious this is the most powerful party. But the Communists are slowly gaining ground as more and more of the population, through unemployment and poverty, seek to change the social structure of the island by a change of government. There is a bitter saying in Sicily: 'Outside the Roman Church there is no salvation, outside the Communist party there is no progress.'

Traditionally Sicily has 4 rulers: the Church, the State (no Sicilian would dream of seeking employment without a recommendation from either his priest or Member of Parliament), the police and the *Mafia*. These institutions between them have turned the once prosperous island into a place of poverty, crime and despair.

THE MAFIA

The *Mafia* is Western Sicily's secret mutual aid society, known to its members as the 'Honoured Society'. *Mafia* is an Arabic word meaning 'place of refuge'.

Before the Normans came to the island it was governed by the Arabs who brought with them their own advanced civilisation. They built irrigation channels to water the barren interior, and created small-holdings for themselves.

If the Arabs had remained, Sicily would be a prosperous island today. Unfortunately, they were subdued by the Normans who imposed their feudal system upon the people, and small-holders were forced to become serfs on the large estates.

To avoid oppression many Sicilian families fled to the mountainous interior, to the *Mafia*—places of refuge—where they held out against their Norman masters, living the life of outlaws and banding together into private armies to resist their conquerors, levying their own form of taxation independent of the Normans. Beyond the jurisdiction of the Norman barons' courts and torture chambers, they created their own system of keeping law and order. Having no prisons or law courts, they always sentenced the guilty to death, even for the smallest offence.

This situation eventually led to the *vendetta*, defined by the Concise Oxford Dictionary as 'the hereditary blood feud in which the family of a murdered man sought vengeance on the murderer or his family'. A vendetta can be carried on through many generations by the hot-blooded Sicilians, ending only with the destruction of a complete family. A man will sometimes wait 30 years to have his revenge, often remaining good friends with the man he will eventually kill. The vendetta can span continents: a shooting in Palermo can be followed up by a knifing in New York.

In the middle of the nineteenth century, during the Spanish conquest of the island, the authorities used armed guards to keep the peace. Many of these were convicted murderers set free on the understanding that they would help the government. Their methods were brutal and bloodthirsty. The Sicilians lost all faith in authority and during this time another Sicilian characteristic emerged: the silence known as *omerta* (manliness). Like the three wise monkeys, Sicilians were expected to see no evil, hear no evil and speak no evil. It became the ultimate sin to report a fellow countryman to the brutal oppressors, in spite of what the man might have done. Later this was extended to all authority, both good and bad alike. Carried to its illogical conclusion a dying man will never reveal his murderer: 'If I die may God forgive me, as I forgive the one who did this. If I manage to pull through I know how to settle my own accounts'.

Because of *omerta* the police have to use stern measures to fight the lawbreakers. When a crime is committed (a robbery, a cattle theft or a vendetta killing), the police round up everyone in the area where the crime took place, young and old alike. They are imprisoned and questioned one by one. The obviously innocent are released the next day. The rest are questioned more carefully, and the innocent are again released, until only a handful of those that did not satisfy the police examiners are left. These are tortured by methods that would make a fish talk, until the real culprit is found. Innocent people often become the victims of this rough justice. One man was almost flogged to death before his innocence was established. He spent weeks in hospital recovering from the broken ribs he had received under torture. There was no redress for this man; he was only a humble peasant, with no influential friends to help him.

The Mafia families began to enjoy their hard-won authority and during more peaceful times they were reluctant to hand over to the government the power and money they had acquired. They came down from the mountains but they did not disband. They continued to dominate by convincing the absentee landlords that their estates needed protecting—

from the Mafia itself. A 'friend', as they like to call themselves, would visit the landowner and offer his services. He would demand to be taken on as a member of the landowner's staff, and, for a handsome fee, would guarantee that the estate would remain free from interference. This system became known as 'wetting the beak'. Most of the landowners agreed to the Mafia's requests: those who did not had their vines pulled down, their buildings burned to the ground and their cattle stolen.

Whenever a robbery was planned, a 'friend' would tell his superiors the number of watchmen on guard at the time planned for the crime. The Mafia would then send an adequate force to deal with any resistance. The watchmen would be overpowered and the cattle driven away to be handed over to other 'friends' in a different part of the island. If the landowner continued to hold out against them, the animals would be quietly shipped across to Naples for distribution to various parts of Italy; or, if the 'friend' took a fancy to them himself, he simply changed the colour of their hides by keeping them for two or three months in a darkened stable. If he wanted to sell them locally where they might be recognised, he changed their appearance still further by soaking a cloth in a soapy solution and then binding it tightly on to the skin, giving the animals new markings and fresh identities. Some animals have been changed so much that after five years of such treatment they are totally unrecognizable as the beasts that were stolen. If the landowner submits, his animals are returned to him, but not directly: they are usually set free on someone else's land, and when caught they are handed over to the police who have a list of all stolen property.

One under the 'protection' of the Mafia, the landowners would find escaped convicts, thieves and known murderers on their payrolls. They would turn a blind eye to the deeds of these men, indifferent to the terror they caused in the community so long as their own property remained unmolested. In return for this 'protection' the landowner was expected to ignore their crimes against others, protect them from the authorities, ensure that they were never convicted in a court of law, and pay them considerable sums of money.

This offer of protection spread outwards from the estates eventually embracing all walks of life; and because the Mafia is such a secret society, so diverse in its activities, and feared by everyone, the police are powerless to protect the private individual. People found that they were paying two separate taxes, one to the Government and the other to the Mafia.

The Mafia does not look upon itself as a criminal organization. Its members consider that they are performing a public service. Under their 'protection' one is guaranteed against all forms of crime. The Sicilian police are ineffective in 75% of the cases brought to their notice and 15% of the thieves caught are found to be working for others and the stolen property is not returned. At best there is only a 10% chance of retrieving one's stolen property lawfully, and then trials can be long drawn out affairs, and the travelling involved to and from court can be costly. Whereas the Mafia, because of its widespread connections, soon apprehends a thief and ensures the return of the stolen property to its rightful owner. The Mafia guarantees a 95% certainty of regaining lost property quickly and efficiently for a fee of one third the value of the goods stolen. Alongside the inadequacy of the police in these matters this is commendation enough to most Sicilians.

The Mafia have no qualms about committing murder to 'keep the peace' or protect their own interests. After all, death can so easily be avoided, it is only the stubborn people who get hurt. The Mafia killings are done by junior members of the Society anxious to please their elders. If there are no juniors available, they hire assassins at £130 a time. The murders are committed with sawn-off shotguns.

Those who have defied the Mafia, if they are lucky enough to escape its vengeance, make for the mountains, where they join the ever-swelling ranks of outlaws and bandits.

Since its beginnings the Mafia has only been silenced once: that was during the period of Mussolini's dictatorship when island prisons were specially constructed to house the Mafiosi rounded up in the Duce's anti-Mafia campaign.

At the end of the second world war the Mafia came back with the allies' blessing and within days half the towns in Sicily had new mayors who were members of the Mafia or in league with it.

Today it is as strong as ever. It does not broadcast itself as much as it once did and there have been fewer Mafia crimes since 1963, but it is no less active—it has just learned to be more discrete.

The Mafia is divided into two groups: the higher Mafia, or *Capi Mafia* (singular *Capo Mafia*) who make all the plans, and the lower Mafia, the juniors, who carry them out. When a group bands together to terrorize the defenceless, each person becomes stronger with the help of his 'friends'. As the old Mafia dictum has it: 'If a man is to be a man he must be stronger than a man.' This man is the Capo Mafia, and because in Sicily you are respected by the amount of fear that you can generate in others, the Capi Mafia are held in high esteem. They may be lawyers, aristocrats, landowners, or even Members of Parliament.

It is from these people that the Head of the Mafia is chosen. In the old days there were savage feuds as Capi Mafia struggled amongst themselves year after year to gain the leadership of the Society. Today things are done much more quietly.

The Head of the Mafia is a well-loved and respected figure. He considers himself a pillar of the community, is usually a keen church-goer, an ideal family man, and generous in the extreme. He is reliable, honest and always loyal to his friends —a man of character, a man of his word. He settles disputes and defines the territories granted to his members, demanding unswerving loyalty and absolute silence (omerta) from them in return. In times of peace they help each other; in times of trouble they unite to fight the common enemy.

Membership is passed on from father to son, but outsiders gain admittance if they possess some special quality or ability which the Society needs. There are no special signs, no dis-distinctive handshakes, no passwords, only a simple initiation ceremony to be gone through in which each new member pricks his finger and lets some of his blood drip on to a picture of a saint. The bloodstained paper is then burned and the applicant, holding the ashes in his hand, swears 'to be loyal to my brothers, never betray them, always to aid them, and if I fail may I burn and be turned to ashes like the ashes of the image'. From now on he is a man of respect, a friend of friends, ready to blackmail, steal, kidnap, run protection rackets, engage in murder and extortion, to raise funds and to assist the 'Honoured Society'.

It is unfortunate, but it pays most Sicilians to keep in with the Mafia. The father of a medical student worried about his final examinations will explain his son's position to a 'friend' who will 'persuade' his professors to pass him. The young doctor now has a debt of gratitude to repay. One good turn deserves another. In return he will be expected to sign false certificates of blindness for people going to the polls. This enables Mafia thugs to accompany them to make sure that they vote for the 'right' candidate. Or, the doctor may be visited at his surgery by a 'friend' suffering from gunshot wounds who needs medical attention—no questions asked. A politician who desperately needs votes at a forthcoming election has this arranged for him by the Society. Once in Parliament, the new M.P. is expected to use his influence to defend 'friends' in trouble, or block a dam project that will endanger the livelihood of another 'friend'. The Mafia can arrange anything: a backward boy can suddenly begin to do very well at school, a bank manager extend credit to a customer with a large overdraft, and criminals are successfully hidden from the police and shipped out to Africa without papers.

The evil influence of the Mafia has spread like oil on water all over western Sicily. Even beggars have their Mafia contacts who ensure that their pitches remain free from intruders.

Since the war there has grown up a more ruthless type of Mafioso usually engaged in the illegal drug trade, one of the areas that was definitely taboo to the highly moral Capo Mafia of the older generation. The new Mafioso feels no loyalty towards the other 'friends'; his primary concern is to 'wet his own beak'. He feels that the days when the Mafia was a mutual aid Society are over.

This then is the Mafia, as active today as it ever was: busy 'wetting its beak' and silencing all those who stand in its way, all those who are for progress and change, all those who threaten its settled livelihood—rivals, communists, trade union leaders, and social reformers like Danilo Dolci.

DANILO DOLCI

Danilo Dolci was born in 1924 in the Italian town of Sesana which is now a part of Yugoslavia. His father was an employee of the Italian State Railways and in 1939 was sent as stationmaster to the Sicilian town of Trappeto, a position

he held until 1942. Danilo did not go with his father but
stayed behind in Italy to complete his education. He visited
his father during the holidays and took a special interest in the
ruined Greek temples scattered throughout the island. At
school Danilo became fascinated by the life and teachings of
the great Indian leader Mahatma Gandhi. Gandhi's ideals of
non-violence and passive resistance were to play a large part
in Danilo's life later on.

The Second World War broke out while he was still at
school, and, because of his pacifist views, he refused to serve as
a soldier in the Italian Army. He was imprisoned, but managed to escape, fleeing to the south where the British and
American troops were driving back the retreating remnants
of Mussolini's once-proud army. For a while he joined the
partisans in the mountains, but, sickened by the senseless
violence that he saw, he threw away his revolver in disgust.

After the war he enrolled as a student of architecture and
engineering at the Universities of Rome and Milan. He
took part in the gay social life of Rome, a city that was just
beginning to find its feet again after the bitter war years.
He mixed with the high society and became engaged to the
daughter of a prosperous building contractor. He was assured
of a partnership in the firm when he left University.

During this time he read an article describing the work of
Roman Catholic Priest Don Zeno Saltini who had turned a
disused concentration camp at Nomadelfia, near Modena in
Northern Italy, into a home for Roman Catholic children
orphaned by the war. Danilo visited Nomadelfia and was most
impressed by what he saw.

Back in Rome he began to think seriously of his future. Did
he really want to become an architect and build bigger and
better houses, swimming pools, and offices, for people who
had adequate accommodation already? Swimming pools, and

houses costing £10,000 and upwards, seemed an extravagant luxury in a world where many people had not so much as a roof over their heads. It seemed unjust.

He decided to leave university, give up all thoughts of taking a degree, turn his back on the world of expensive sports cars and endless all-night parties, and . . . What? He decided that the would dedicate his life to helping the poor. He would go to Nomadelfia and assist Don Zeno. After all, he needed houses far more desperately than the millionaires in Rome. But there was his family to consider.

YOU'RE A FOOL, SON

CHARACTERS: *Danilo's father*
               Danilo

SCENE: Dolci's home.

1. Danilo's father is reading a newspaper.

2. Danilo arrives home. His father is not expecting him. He asks Danilo why he is not at the University. Danilo tells him that he has decided to leave the University before taking his final examination and that he has broken off his engagement.

3. His father is furious. All the money that has been spent on his education has been wasted. He had seen marvellous prospects for his son: a partnership in his future father-in-law's firm, a rich wife, an expensive house, a family . . . and now, through his stupidity—nothing. He tells Danilo of his own struggle for promotion, how difficult it had been; by comparison Danilo has had it handed to him on a plate. Why has he been such a fool?

4. Danilo tries to explain his thoughts—his desire to do something for the poor, Nomadelfia, the ragged urchins so desperately in need of help. But his father will not listen. There are rich people and there are poor people; that is the way of the world and no amount of help is going to change it. His father storms out of the room.

Danilo went to Nomadelfia and became Don Zeno's secretary. The former concentration camp was full to overflowing with 1400 Catholic orphans in the care of 60 adults. 3000 other orphans waited outside the gates in the hope of getting in. The situation was impossible.

Danilo started a small orchestra with some of the children, others went off to fell trees. Anything to keep the children busy, stop them thinking, stop them becoming bored.

Don Zeno was continually in debt, but somehow he managed to keep Nomadelfia going. He commissioned Danilo to build a small village, just a church, a school, and 11 houses to ease the overcrowding at the camp. Danilo and some of the older boys worked 18 hours a day and the village gradually began to take shape.

There was much unemployment in the area and several unemployed labourers asked Danilo if he would take them on to help with the work. Danilo agreed. When Don Zeno heard of this, he was furious.

WHAT DO YOU THINK THIS IS? A LABOUR EXCHANGE?

CHARACTERS: *Don Zeno Saltini*
                        Danilo

SCENE: Don Zeno's office at Nomadelfia.

1. Don Zeno is seated at his desk trying to balance his accounts.

2. Danilo enters and asks why Don Zeno has sent for him. Don Zeno tells Danilo that he is not running a labour exchange and he must stop giving work to the labourers outside the camp.

3. Danilo argues that they are hungry and have wives and families of their own to support. Don Zeno replies that they are Communists. He is running Nomadelfia for the benefit of Catholics only. (*Bring into your argument any relevant information that you discovered in your researches into the differences between Catholics and Communists.*)

4. Danilo tells Don Zeno that he is not concerned with the differences between Catholics and Communists. They are all men, and as far as he is concerned they are entitled to work.

5. Don Zeno once more forbids Danilo to employ them. By this time Danilo is very angry. He refuses to accept Don Zeno's ban on Communists and he storms out threatening to employ as many of the labourers as he can regardless of their ideologies.

Don Zeno sinks further into debt and all the work on the village has to stop. His attitude towards the unemployed labourers continues to annoy Danilo and in the end he can stand the tension no longer. He breaks with Don Zeno and leaves Nomadelfia.

Where to go now? He remembered Trappeto, the place where he had holidayed with his parents. 'The poorest place on earth', his Father had called it. Perhaps he could be of some help there.

When he got off the 1 p.m. train in Trappeto in 1952, he was 28 years old and had 4d. in his pocket. A young Sicilian recognized him as the former stationmaster's son. For want of something better to do, they went for a walk around the town.

Trappeto had a population of 2800 and lies 22 miles west of the capital city of Palermo. Down through the centre of the town ran an open canal, called the *Vallone*. Its foul smelling waters served as a drain, a sewer, a rubbish tip and a playground for the hordes of ragged children found along its banks. At times the fetid waters overflowed and trickled into the back streets, seeping into the houses.

For most of the large families, home was one small room roughly 16 feet square with a floor of beaten earth.

In 1952 it was a place of indescribable poverty. Only 10 families had running water, the rest drew their daily supply from a contaminated well. There were no water closets, no electricity, no telephones and very little work. The labourers were lucky if they got 90 days' work in a year. The fishermen had virtually been driven from the seas by pirate trawlers operated by the Mafia. Some men had never worked in their lives. To bring in extra money to feed their families, men searched along the railway lines for coal that had fallen off the locomotives and sold it to wandering tinkers, and to bakers for their ovens. Others hunted for the spent bullets on the police firing ranges. The lead could be sold—lead for bread. Selling the aluminium casings from exploded police grenades was another source of income. Many went out with their donkeys on long journeys into the mountains to cut *disa* for making brooms. If the disa was too dry it was mixed with straw and exchanged for bread at the local bakeries where it was used as fuel for the ovens. The rate was eight bundles of disa for $4\frac{1}{2}$ pounds weight of bread, the wages for a long and exhausting day's work. Some men managed to earn a little money selling wild asparagus, turnips, cauliflowers, plants such as fennel for making sauces, and chicory leaves for salads. Snails were caught and sold to the housewives to be boiled down into a thick stew that was eaten with tomato sauce.

Very few of the children had been to school for more than a year—many had never been at all. Their parents could not afford to buy the text books and uniforms. Employers too hindered the children's education by providing boys with work at the rate of 4/4d. per day. This was cheap labour compared with the 11/- a day they had to pay the boys' fathers. An unemployed parent preferred to send his son out to work to earn money to feed the rest of his family than to send him to school where he earned nothing.

Poverty was encouraged by the unwillingness of the people to adopt new methods and ideas. Potatoes, carrots, and lettuces, had to be imported from Italy because the people would not grow them themselves in spite of the shipping charges that added considerably to their cost.

The Trappetans are extremely superstitious. A farm labourer discovered a crippled toad that had been run over by a farm cart. He bandaged its bleeding leg with his handkerchief and placed it by the side of the road out of harm's way to recover. Later that day he was greeted by a woman calling his name. She led him back to her house, returned his handkerchief, and told him that she was the toad he had rescued earlier in the day. She was exceedingly grateful.

They place great faith in witchcraft: fishermen cast spells on their rivals boats to ensure that they return empty-handed.

Faithhealers are constantly in demand with their strange medieval remedies. Eye-diseases are said to be cured by rubbing the infected parts with the green slime found on the stagnant waters of public drinking troughs; the saliva of cows and mules, dissolved in water, is used in the treatment of trachoma. Young children with stomach-ache are given milk to which fly droppings have been added. Raw tortoise blood is highly thought of for its medicinal properties.

Men make a living using leeches to cure the sick. These fresh-water blood-sucking worms are bought in Palermo and as many as twenty at a time are placed behind the ears of patients suffering from sun-stroke, meningitis, diphtheria, sprains, typhus, and heart attacks, or between the shoulders and on the chest for those with tuberculosis. They are even used on week-old babies.

If the quack doctor ran out of leeches he sent for the local barber who opened up a vein to let out the necessary blood. Barbers were sent for rather than doctors because they were cheaper, asking only a taken payment of 100 lire (roughly 1/-), whereas a doctor would charge anything from 500 to 1000 lire (5/- to 10/-).

Because of their lack of education the people are ignorant of the world outside. One person thought that China was a kind of grape, while another had always pictured Russia as being a small island.

Danilo was shocked by what he saw. Here indeed were a people desperately in need of help. He stopped to talk with a group of unemployed labourers. One told him that a vet would condemn his house as unfit for a pig to live in let alone a human being. Another said, 'If we hadn't been baptized we'd be no better than talking animals'. 'When our babies cry we steal for them', said a third. 'But have you no land?' asked Danilo. 'Yes, six feet of it in the cemetery when we're dead', was the sarcastic reply. To the question 'What do you want more than anything else in the world?', the answer was always the same: 'Work'.

They began to get suspicious as Danilo questioned them still further. They asked whose side he was on, the Communists or the Democrats. Danilo told them he was on neither side; he had come to live among them, to share their lives, and to build a home where the poorest of them could be looked after. He wanted to help people like Rosetta, an 8-year-old girl compelled to sleep with her father, who was suffering from tuberculosis, because the family only had one bed. They would all live together like brothers, he told them, and help each other. He confessed that he had no money with which to carry out his ideas, but he would raise it somehow or other; and in the meantime he would teach them to help themselves.

A farmer offered Danilo a site for his home for £120 and three days later he set off on a fund-raising tour of Northern Italy, collecting £60 from his University Professor which he put down as a deposit on his plot of land. Danilo gave the owner a signed agreement to pay the other £60 later. He put up a tent to live in and began to draw up the plans for his future home.

He soon discovered that many sick people in Trappeto were being denied proper medical treatment because they could not afford to buy medicine. There was no Chemist shop in Trappeto; the nearest one was in Balestrate, the next town. Danilo became a regular customer at this shop, collecting the prescriptions for his patients, paying the chemist if he had any money, and obtaining the supplies on credit if not. If the chemist refused to serve him he would visit people in the town and ask them if they could spare him any of the medicines he needed. He bought himself a scooter so that he could travel around more quickly.

But in spite of Danilo's help there were the tragedies.

One day, while he was out walking with his friend Franco, he was called to a basement home close to the Vallone.

MURDER BY NEGLECT

CHARACTERS: *Danilo*
Franco—his friend
Justina Barretta—a 22-year-old mother
A doctor

SCENE: Justina's basement home. The sewer waters of the Vallone have seeped through the walls leaving dark stains on the crumbling stone work. The only piece of furniture is a mattress placed upon wooden boards resting on an iron support. Justina is nursing her baby which is only a few weeks old. It is very cold and dark inside the room.

1. Danilo and Franco enter. Justina tells them that she is worried about her baby. It is her first child and she has no milk for it. Apart from a slice of bread and some *pasta* that one of the neighbours gave her, the baby has had nothing to eat for days. The poor little creature is starving.

2. Danilo tells Justina that he will go out and get some powdered milk.

3. While he is away Franco tries to comfort Justina as best he can.

4. Danilo comes back with the powdered milk made up in a bottle. He takes the child from its mother and pushes the

teat into the baby's mouth; but the baby cannot take the food and is violently sick.

5. Danilo puts the child on the bed and sends Franco for the doctor. While Danilo and Justina wait the baby dies. Danilo cannot believe it—that a child can be allowed to die of hunger in a Christian country in 1952.

6. The mother is too weak to respond. She does not cry. She just sits and gazes at the little corpse in shocked bewilderment; her hair is wild with grief, her face yellow through malnutrition.

6. The doctor arrives and Danilo tells him the bitter news.

7. This is murder if anything is—'murder by neglect'.

8. Danilo and Franco go out into the fresh air leaving the doctor to fill in the death certificate.

(*Write down your thoughts after acting this scene. Write it as a poem if you wish.*)

On the following Sunday a crowd of people including the Mayor and the Archpriest of Balestrate came out to see what Danilo was doing. When he explained that he was going to build a home for the poor they were most enthusiastic and offered to help him in any way they could. Later when he needed assistance, the priest made the excuse that he was only interested in people's souls, and the Mayor, when asked if he could do anything about the broken drains on the adjoining land, explained that they were none of his business.

With the help of a local mason and two labourers, Danilo began building his home. He obtained mortar and lime on credit and the money to pay for the stone was provided by friends in Italy. Money always seemed to turn up when it was needed. Even the miserly local assistance board helped him out with funds when he most needed them.

The building was completed within two months and practically everybody in Trappeto came to the opening ceremony. After all, it was the only building in the town with a bath. Danilo called it *Borgo di Dio*—The Hamlet of God.

The first people to move in were Justina Barretta and her husband. All in need were welcome. Danilo did not discriminate: he took the children whose parents had been killed by outlaws along with those of their murderers. The needy, the desperate, the pathetic, all were taken in. The children found it more difficult than the adults to adjust to their new way of life. If they were given a loaf of bread some of them would hide half of it away for the next day; they had not yet realized that each day brought a fresh supply of food.

The day after the opening Vincenzina, a widow, came with her five children and accompanied by her mother and father-in-law. Her husband had only recently been killed by bandits. She stayed on to become Borgo's housekeeper and, later, Danilo's wife.

There was a continual stream of orphans asking to be admitted to Borgo, and the home was soon full up. Danilo had to turn many away.

When the unemployed labourers and fishermen heard that Danilo was considering building a road up to Borgo, he was inundated with offers of work. He took on 20 men, explaining that because of lack of funds he would not be able to pay them straight away, but when he obtained some more money they would receive their wages. Gradually this labour force grew to 40, as desperate men grabbed at the chance of working for a while to earn money for their families and dignity for themselves. The local shopkeepers, trusting Danilo, let the men have goods on credit. This encouraged others to come to Borgo seeking work. When the road was completed he kept them on to dig over the waste ground around Borgo. Eventually eighty men a day had to be turned away as every available square inch of soil was being dug and re-dug by Danilo's labourers desperate to remain in work.

All the furniture at Borgo had been bought on credit. Danilo was always intending to pay for it when he had money available, but other things always seemed more important: paying his 40 road-builders, or obtaining medicine for the sick. But the owner of the shop that supplied the furniture became tired of waiting for his money and sent two of his strongarm boys to Borgo to persuade Danilo to settle his account.

PAY UP OR WE'LL BASH YOUR BRAINS OUT!

CHARACTERS: *Danilo*
  Carlo
  Angelo } *furniture shop employees*

SCENE: Danilo's room at Borgo.

1. Danilo is sitting at his desk writing a letter.

2. Carlo and Angelo burst in. They tell him that they are from the furniture shop and have come to collect the payment on the furniture. They threaten to take it away if he does not pay up.

3. Danilo tries to explain that he is short of money at the moment; he has to pay his 40 labourers, buy medicines, etc. He promises to pay as soon as funds are available.

4. The men become angry. They seize him by the jacket and shake him, shouting, 'Pay us the money or we'll bash your brains out!'

5. Danilo is a big man and he could easily fight them off, but his pacifist principles will not let him resort to violence. 'Coward! Swindler!' they scream. They talk of taking Danilo to Palermo and handing him over to the police.

6. Danilo protests that if they do this the children at Borgo will starve. He has no money now; he will pay them later. They are not satisfied and continue to shout and threaten him. Then he remembers his scooter. He mentions it to the men, asking them if they will accept it as security against his debt. They grudgingly agree.

7. Danilo fetches the scooter and the men wheel it away warning him that they will be back if the money is not paid in the near future.

Four months later Danilo obtained the money and claimed back his scooter. He still deals with the same shop!

During this time he began to write the first of a series of of reports on the living conditions in western Sicily which were to make him world-famous. Some families, he discovered, were existing on as little as 7d. a day. The Mafia demanded £1200 from an elderly farmer, and when he refused to pay up, they hacked down his vines, killed his mule, and left a note threatening him with death if he returned to his property. They fired several rounds of ammunition at the house of another farmer to force him into paying protection money.

It did not take Danilo long to work out a solution to the unemployment problem. The answer lay in harnessing the waters of the local river. Each year the Iato flowed through a dry and barren wilderness on its journey to the sea, its life-giving waters lost for ever in the Mediterranean. If the authorities could be persuaded to build a dam above the Taurro bridge to hold back the Iato's vital waters, and install one 40 h.p. pump to transfer these waters onto the parched land, then 20,000 acres of wilderness could be changed overnight into productive farmland giving work to the unemployed and bringing prosperity to the whole region.

Danilo went to the Regional Authorities at the Town Hall with his plan, but they were unimpressed. 7 to 8 hundred million lire (the cost of such a scheme) was too large a price to pay for a handful of peasants. Danilo was furious. This amount of money was being spent each year by these same authorities in order to maintain a substantial police force for the suppression of banditry in the area—banditry that was caused as a direct result of unemployment. Transfer that money over to build a dam and there would be no unemployment, no banditry, and hence no need for the police. The Mafia too had a hand in obstructing Danilo's plans. They were making easy money from the sale of water provided by their artesian wells, and an irrigation system would soon put a stop to this profitable sideline. When Danilo next went to the Town Hall he was told that the official in charge was on holiday and his secretary was nowhere to be found. The man on the door was deliberately obstructive.

Desperate conditions call for desperate remedies. At a meeting held on October 14th, 1952, Danilo described to his friends the process by which a seed has to die in order to produce new life. If by living he could achieve nothing for them then he must die, and perhaps through his death the Regional Authorities might be made to wake up to their responsibilities. He told his friends that he was going on a hunger strike. He would not eat again until 30 million lire had been provided by the authorities to help the needy. His friends resolved that if he died they too would follow his example so that there would be a continuous protest of death.

Before Danilo began his hunger strike he wrote a letter to his friends all over Italy explaining his purpose. (*Write the kind of letter you think he would have written. Begin 'To all my friends'. Don't forget to include details of the terrible conditions in Trappeto and Danilo's plan for ending unemployment.*)

The next day Danilo, accompanied by Franco, his friend, went to Justina's house down by the Vallone and there he stretched himself out on her old straw mattress and began to die. Almost immediately a policeman took up a position outside. The police were to keep a twenty-four-hour watch on the house. His friends took over the running of Borgo.

The people of Trappeto were shocked to hear what Danilo was doing.

THE DYING SEED

CHARACTERS: *Danilo*
                Franco
                Justina Barretta
                Vincenzina—Borgo's housekeeper
                A crowd of Trappetans

SCENE: Justina's old home.

1. Danilo asks Franco for a glass of water, the only nourishment he is allowing himself. The door opens and in comes Justina, Vincenzina and a crowd of Trappetans. They try to persuade him to eat. They tell him that he must not starve himself for them. It is wrong.

T.D.O.—E

2. Danilo comforts them. He is content and in good spirits.

3. Franco asks them to leave as Danilo is rather tired and he must not have too much excitement.

4. They leave. Franco goes for the glass of water.

At first, the authorities ignored him; they did not for one moment believe that he would go through with it. But after four days they began to show concern.

MORE THAN YOU CAN CHEW

CHARACTERS: *Franco*
Danilo
Doctor Mignesi (Secretary to Alessi, an important Sicilian M.P.)

SCENE: Justina's house.

1. Franco sits beside Danilo. They talk very little, each occupied with his own thoughts.

2. There is a knock at the door. Franco opens it and in walks Doctor Mignesi. He introduces himself as Alessi's secretary and Franco introduces Danilo.

3. Doctor Mignesi tries to persuade Danilo to call off his hunger strike, telling him that he has bitten off more than he can chew.

4. Danilo replies that someone has to die before anything will be done.

5. Doctor Mignesi tells Danilo that if he wants things done there are other ways of going about it.

6. Danilo explains that he has tried other ways. He has been to the Town Hall, for example, but he has had no success. Justina's baby died of hunger; there is no money for medicine; men and women walk the streets in deperation, their faces grey with worry because there is no food for their children; old men of 70 and over still have to go out to work to support their families on the pittance that they are paid; many widows are bringing up their families with no help from the State; men in hospital worry day and night because they have left their families unprovided for; and men are imprisoned for stealing food for their starving children—long prison sentences are no cure for poverty.

7. Doctor Mignesi is embarrassed by Danilo's speech. He excuses himself on the grounds that he is rather busy. He will see what can be done, but he doubts whether he will be able to raise much money himself. As he walks out of the door, Danilo tells him that 1000 lire will do for a start.

8. He drives off in his car and Franco goes back to his anxious vigil.

Justina and Vincenzina managed to get away from Borgo for a short time each day. They put on a brave face when they were with Danilo, but they cried openly in the streets when they left him.

On the seventh day Danilo had a stroke. Franco sent for the doctor who examined him and found that his heart beat was irregular, his pulse weak, and his right leg and hand half-paralysed. He was in very bad shape. The doctor was annoyed and after giving him an injection of camphor drops to prolong his heart beat he demanded that Danilo give up this foolish behaviour immediately. But Danilo continued to die.

On the eighth day Franco went to Doctor Mignesi to inform him that Danilo's heart beat was getting weaker—he had not long to live.

The authorities had underestimated their man. Danilo was becoming a well-known figure through his report on the social conditions. They could not let him die. They must do something—quickly.

THE NEW CORN BEGINS TO GROW

CHARACTERS: *Danilo*
             Franco
             First representative of the Regional Government
             Second representative
             Third representative
             People of Trappeto
             A spokesman

SCENE 1: Justina's house.

1. Franco sits with Danilo. He is very weak now.

2. There is a knock on the door. Franco opens it and the three representatives enter. They introduce themselves.

3. The first representative tells Danilo that they all realize how poverty-stricken Trappeto really is. In view of this, the Regional Government is going to arrange homes for the most needy amongst the children and old people.

4. The second representative tells him that the Government has agreed to pay for the dam and $1\frac{1}{2}$ million lire is available at once so that work can be started immediately.

5. The third representative speaks of a further 5 million lire that is being donated to improve the road surfaces. The scheme will provide training in road-making techniques and work for 67 unemployed labourers and fisherfolk.

6. Danilo asks them if they would mind if he discussed their proposals privately with his friends. They agree and withdraw. Danilo tells Franco to fetch all his friends for a very important meeting.

SCENE 2: The same some time later.

1. Danilo is alone. The door opens quietly and Franco and his friends enter the room.

2. Danilo outlines the scheme put forward by the three representatives from the Government. He asks them to consider the proposals very carefully. Do they agree to them or would they prefer something better? They are not to agree just to save his life. If they are not satisfied he will carry on with his hunger strike.

3. One of the men acts as a spokesman. He points out to Danilo that he is starving himself for 30 million lire, whereas the authorities have agreed to pay for the dam, which will cost 60 million; besides, they have said that they will look after the needy and surface the roads at the same time. They are getting a far better bargain than they had hoped for in their wildest dreams.

4. Danilo agrees with them. He asks Franco to fetch back the three representatives.

Within two days Danilo was eating normally again and back organizing the work at Borgo. Preparations began for work on the dam, and foreign visitors began to arrive. They had read Danilo's report and had come to see for themselves the work that he was doing. Some came only for a short visit, while others stayed on to help. Others, who had read the report but could not afford the fare, sent medicines, food and powdered milk.

Early in 1953 the first telephone was installed in Trappeto, a chemist's shop was opened, drains were laid, and a large sum of money was spent resurfacing the muddy streets.

Later that same year Danilo and Vincenzina were married.

Danilo next turned his attention to the problem of the pirate fishing boats which were driving the local fishermen from their homes. Owned by large business syndicates and supported by the Mafia, these modern well-equipped trawlers were far superior to the small boats owned by the local fishermen; but, to destroy any chance that the local people may have had of competing with them, they turned to underhand methods, using bombs, chemicals, and nets with very fine mesh to obtain their catches. Sailing within the three-mile limit, sometimes as close as 60 yards from the shore, 2 to 8 trawlers exploded 20 to 30 bombs a day between April and October (the sea is too rough for fishing in winter) under the waters of the Gulfs of Castellamare and Selinunte.

The pirates ignite the fuses on their bombs with lighted cigarette ends, then heave them over the side as far down-current as they can to avoid scaring the fish away before the explosion. The fuse flares under the water and dies out; then the bomb explodes, blasting some of the fish right out of the water and on to the decks of the pirate vessels. The pirates lower their nets and draw in as much as 4 tons of fish in one catch—sardines, mackerel, anchovies, and tuna. Nothing is heard on land if the pirates anchor well out to sea, but if they sail close in-shore the explosions can sound like a naval bombardment.

In the early days, before they became familiar with the use of explosives, one crew blew up their boat. The stone weight came off as they cast the bomb over the side. Instead of sinking, the bomb floated back towards the ship and exploded, stoving in the side and capsizing the crew into the waters of the Gulf. Unfortunately for the local fishermen, the pirates have now learned to control their 100-gramme charges of dynamite with deadly accuracy.

The nets used by the local fishermen have meshes wide enough to permit the young fish to escape, but the nets used by the pirates have a much finer mesh which traps not only the adult fish but the young fry as well, sometimes even scraping up the fishes' eggs from the bottom of the sea. There are roughly 2500 to 3000 small fish in just over 2 pounds of sardine fry; if left, these can develop into 154 pounds of fully-grown fish which can in turn spawn a further 1540 pounds of fish in one season. Therefore, by selling the fry, the pirates are robbing the local fishermen of shoals of fish every year. In spite of a law forbidding it, sardine fry are sold openly on the Palermo market.

The pirates also use potassium in their endeavours to net as many fish as possible with the minimum of effort. Potassium can be bought ready made up as a stain-remover. The pirates lower their nets, then throw a quantity of the chemical into the water in small lumps no larger than an aspirin tablet. It dissolves within minutes changing the colour of the sea to a milky white and blinding all the fish within range. The fish, robbed of their sight, are easily caught in the encircling nets of the pirate trawlers. When bombs are used, the fish that survive are frightened away by the noise of the explosion, but they return after a day or two; when potassium is used, it takes many storms to dissipate the smell and it is many months before the surviving fish come back.

8000 people have had their livelihood taken away by 7 or 8 of these unscrupulous pirates, who could at most be supporting only 200 people on the £50 to £100 per trawler per day that they are earning from the sale of the pirated fish.

Every bomb thrown makes one fisherman redundant. Three shillings worth of fish was the total amount caught by the crew of one boat whose earnings were shared out among 16 families. One quarter of the Italian fishing-fleet is registered in Sicily, and Italy is losing £7000 worth of fish annually in the Gulf of Castellamare alone because of the pirates.

The piracy goes on openly right under the noses of the fully-staffed local customs and excise department and of the police force. A police corporal in Sciacca who tried to put an end to the piracy was suddenly posted to another part of the island. It was rumoured that the authorities were in league with the pirates, or at least that the pirates were informed by radio before the police or the customs cutter appeared on the scene. The police and the customs officials always seemed to take their time in coming when they were told of pirate trawlers in the area.

Hundreds of fishermen used to fish in the Gulf. Today, sickened at heart, they have either left the area or taken up alternative employment. Those who have gone to fish elsewhere do not have the first-hand knowledge of the local winds and tides that is so essential to success; they tear their nets on unfamiliar rocks, and run aground on unknown sandbanks, while their former homes crumble into ruins. Others have begun to throw bombs, use potassium and fish with close-mesh nets in a desperate attempt to keep up with the pirates.

In order to try to get something done, Danilo made a series of notes on the arrivals and departures of the pirate trawlers and sent the information to people in authority both in Sicily and on the Italian mainland.

These letters had some effect; the next time the authorities were informed that there were pirates in the area the customs cutter appeared more quickly than before and caught the illegal trawler inside the three-mile limit. But the local fishermen were sceptical about the result; they felt the customs officials would be bribed with offers of fish, or, if they managed to bring the crew to court, the maximum fine they would dare to impose would only be £5 to £10, a trivial sum compared with the £50 to £100 the pirates were earning each day by breaking the law. The fishermen became so disillusioned that they began to talk of violence as the only answer to their problem.

DEEDS, NOT WORDS

CHARACTERS: *Danilo*
             A crowd of angry fishermen

SCENE: The harbour at Balestrate. A group of local fishermen are standing on the quay. They should be out fishing, but the pirates have completely shattered their hopes of ever again earning a livelihood from the sea. They are disheartened and very bitter.

1. They talk amongst themselves about the pirates, their bombs, their fine nets and their chemicals.

2. Danilo joins them. They tell him of their plight; how many have left the area, how they are having to take up other work —some are elderly and after a lifetime spent at sea it is not easy to make a fresh start—and all this because of the pirates.

3. Danilo explains that he has written to the authorities.

4. The fishermen complain that the authorities have done little to stop the pirates so far. By the time the police arrive the pirates have usually sailed out far beyond the three-mile limit where they are safe from arrest. If they are caught they probably bribe the customs officials and get away with it; and if they are taken to court the fine is so small compared with what they are earning, that it pays them to keep up their piracy. If it was the rich who were involved instead of poor fisherfolk something would soon be done.

5. The fishermen become very angry and one suggested that letter-writing will do no good: arguing will not solve the problem—the time has come for action.

6. The other fishermen quickly take up the challenge: they will take a boat out, board one of the pirate-boats beat up the crew, throw them overboard, cut up their nets and scuttle the ship. This will soon bring in the police: nothing fetches them quicker than a fight. This would lead to an inquiry and at last something might possibly be done about the pirates.

7. Danilo realizes that violence would only breed violence and it would not be the pirates who would lose. But how can he stop these determined men from carrying out their act of revenge?

(*Discuss amongst yourselves ways in which Danilo could talk the men out of their decision to board one of the pirate trawlers, and then finish off the scene yourselves.*)

Danilo wrote a further letter about the pirates to the Port Captain at Palermo. (*Write a copy of the kind of letter that you think Danilo would have written. Begin it:* To The Port Captain, Palermo (or the competent authorities). Sir, . . .)

Their only reply was to sneer at his attempts to rid the Gulf of piracy. He was constantly being told 'You can't beat the Mafia at sea'.

In yet another case of piracy the customs cutter was sent for, but when it appeared the pirates were again well outside the three-mile limit. The captain of the cutter promised he would come back later that day. The fishermen again talked of revenge against the pirates.

The trawler returned and came close in shore; at first they worked without lights, but later, when the customs cutter did not return, the pirates switched on their powerful arc lamps and worked in full view of the watchers on the quay. The audacity of the pirates further convinced the fishermen that they had contacts on land who were keeping a close watch on the police and the customs and reporting their movements back to the pirates by short-wave radio. Unable to stand the tension any longer, several local motor boats full of fishermen set out for the trawler. Danilo went with them.

THE ULTIMATUM

CHARACTERS: *Danilo*
               A crowd of fishermen
               The pirate crew

SCENE (1): The deck of the Balestrate fishing-boat *Carissimo* circling one of the pirate trawlers. (2): The deck of the pirate trawler.

1. The *Carissimo* comes within hailing distance of the trawler.

2. *Carry on the scene yourselves. What shouted conversation takes place between the fishermen and the pirates?* THE FISHERMEN

DO NOT BOARD THE TRAWLER. *End the scene with Danilo telling the pirates that the fishermen are extremely angry and if they do not pull in their nets, weigh anchor and sail away for good, the fishermen will board their trawler, and in a very short time their wives will become widows.*

3. The pirates heed Danilo's warning: they pull in their nets and make for the open sea. The fishermen cheer at the success of their bloodless victory.

The next day the pirates returned. Danilo spent hours trying to telephone the authorities responsible for guarding the rights of the local fishermen. Sometimes they were not available, at other times they were indisposed or there were no boats ready, or he found himself phoning a series of wrong numbers. When he did at last make contact all he got was a string of empty promises. By the end of that year there had only been 15 days in which the pirates had not put in an appearance.

If Danilo had been content just to provide an orphanage there would have been no trouble. But he had twice overstepped the mark: first by publishing an account of the poverty in western Sicily—one should hide one's shame, not broadcast it to the rest of the world—and secondly by interfering in the dispute over the pirates' illegal fishing. He had to be taught a lesson.

Thirty to thirty-five *carabinieri* (police), armed with rifles and machine guns and commanded by a Staff Officer, paid a visit to Borgo.

BORGO DI DIO—TEMPORARILY CLOSED

CHARACTERS: *A party of foreign helpers* (*Decide which country you come from and the kind of work you are doing at Borgo: teaching, nursing, etc.*)

> *A group of orphans*
> *Danilo*
> *A carabinieri Staff Officer*
> *Members of the carabinieri*

SCENE: The Dining Room at Borgo. Danilo, his foreign helpers and the children are just finishing their lunch.

1. The door suddenly bursts open and a *carabinieri* Staff Officer and a party of policemen rush in armed with rifles and machine guns.

2. Some of the children, terrified by what is happening, rush towards the open window and escape into the garden.

3. The Staff Officer orders some of his men to bring them back. He quickly stations the rest of his forces so that Danilo and his friends are unable to escape.

4. Danilo complains to the Staff Officer, who brushes him aside. He asks to see the passports of the foreign helpers. He questions them. What is their nationality? Why have they come to Sicily? What is the nature of their work at Borgo?

5. The *carabinieri* who were sent outside return with the children who tried to escape.

6. The Officer then announces that he is closing Borgo down, and the orphans will all be placed in religious colleges. Danilo asks him the reason for this, but he refuses to give one. He orders Danilo, his staff and children to get packed and ready to leave immediately.

Borgo was re-opened, but Danilo decided to move on. There were several reasons for this. Many people in Trappeto did not take his work there seriously—they thought of Borgo more as a fun palace than a charitable institution. The local fishermen were leaving the area and taking their children with them. The local priest made no attempt to co-operate with Danilo, in fact, he started a school in opposition. Finally, because Danilo had opened Borgo to all-comers, he was suspected of being a Communist, and therefore everything he did was viewed with suspicion.

His friends took over the running of Borgo, and it is now the centre for Danilo's teacher-training courses.

Danilo himself moved on to the *Spine Sante* quarter of Partinico, the most poverty-striken part of the town. The conditions here were even more appalling than they had been in Trappeto. There were the same problems of unemployment: over 28% of the population was out of work for 6 months of the year, and the streets were crowded with heavy-hearted men who mooched aimlessly up and down, broken in mind and body by the grinding squalor in which they lived. The grey, haggard face of wretchedness was to be seen everywhere, but there was more destitution, more uncleanliness—much more. Over one quarter of the streets had no drains and much of the dirty water and slops were thrown out into open channels that had been carved out of the beaten earth by the rivers of black water as they flowed away through the town. Flies swarmed on the rubbish heaps that grew daily until washed away by the rain; if there was an exceptionally heavy downpour the filth was washed into the houses themselves. Occasionally the heaps were removed by roadsweepers and piled up outside the town, but usually they were left to accumulate, becoming the breeding grounds of flies and disease-carrying rats. Hunger was so acute in the

Spine Sante quarter that bones, orange peel, cabbage stalks, in fact anything edible, was quickly removed from these heaps by desperate parents who fed the refuse to their starving families. Trays of tomato preserve were placed outside the houses to dry in the sun amidst the putrid smells of the decaying rubbish. Maltese fever, tuberculosis and dysentry flourished unchecked in the rat-infested slums. Half the population was suffering from tapeworms anything from three to seven feet long. Bedbugs, lice, fleas, bloodsucking mothflies, ticks (from the livestock) and malarial mosquitoes multiplied in this polluted environment.

Families of up to ten people or more lived in crowded one-roomed houses no more than eighteen by fifteen feet in area, a hole in the floor served as a toilet cut off from the rest of the room by a curtain. This room was shared with the livestock (goats, turkeys, donkeys, mules and chickens) because the family had nowhere else to keep them. In the height of summer the windows were all tightly shut—the stuffiness and the smell of the animals was preferable to the nauseating stench of decay outside. A teenage girl with a high temperature brought on by a bad attack of pleurisy slept in a house where the rain seeped in through the roof. Old men, riddled with disease, shared their primitive beds with young babies because there was nowhere else for them to sleep. Sometimes there was no bed and the family had to sleep on the floor. The houses had no damp-courses and pools of water collected on the uneven floors, seeping up from the damp earth underneath.

Few of the people could afford to eat a breakfast. The first meal of the day generally consisted of a hunk of bread eaten early in the afternoon. The main meal of the day was eaten at night and, if the family was very poor, consisted of a plate of snails or shellfish and spaghetti garnished with herbs.

Growing children supplemented their inadequate diet by eating anything they could lay their hands on in the streets.

In order to qualify for a family allowance, a man had to be employed for a certain number of days on the run. This was impossible in the cases of men who had never worked or had only been employed as casual day-labourers; consequently very few were paid out.

Water for washing purposes came direct from a slaughter house where it had been used to clean the dead carcases; it then flowed on to three flour mills where, in spite of the impurities it had picked up on its journey, it was considered suitable for washing grain.

Drinking water was available from a tap whose use was strictly limited to $4\frac{1}{2}$ hours a day, but the earthenware pipe that supplied the water was always fracturing and the fetid water from the open drains seeped in. Women formed long queues, waiting for the water.

Partinico lies in the heart of the Mafia country. Twenty miles away is Corleone with a population of 15,500 and a reputation for murder beyond that of anywhere else of comparable size in the world. 109 inhabitants had lost their lives in the 1914–18 war; 138 had been murdered since the end of World War II. Weapons were easily obtainable—a loaded biretta pistol could be bought for under £10. Life was cheap. Two men were shot by a landowner for collecting their own olives which hung over his property. A man was accused of killing his own brother for £2. Justice was severe: four years' imprisonment for stealing a loaf of bread.

Unemployment had driven many men into lives of lawlessness. At the end of the Second World War thirty separate gangs of heavily armed outlaws terrorized the region and many still remained, making their homes in fortified strongholds in the hills overlooking the town. Periodically they came down to rob and plunder, and terror walked the streets.

Danilo viewed the situation with dismay. If only he could do something about the unemployment. If only there was some way of demonstrating that even in Partinico men could work if given the opportunity.

He found the solution in Article 4 of the Italian Constitution:

'The Republic recognizes the right of all citizens to work and ensures the conditions necessary to render this right effective. . . . It is the duty of every citizen to follow, according to his abilities and his own choice, such calling or profession as shall contribute to the material and spiritual progress of the community.'

Within 2 miles of Partinico there is a 200-yard stretch of country lane known in the neighbourhood as the old track of Valguarneria. The surface had been badly churned up by farm carts during the winter rains, leaving large holes which made transport along it impossible. This was just what Danilo had been looking for. The Italian Constitution stated a citizen's right to work and the farmers wanted the road repaired. Here then was a piece of work to be tackled. Here was work for some of the unemployed. But could it be called work in the true sense of the word? No one would employ them: no one would pay them for repairing it. Danilo realized this, but his intention was not that the labourers should receive money, but that they should demonstrate their ability to work. Workers had the right to strike, to down tools. Danilo held that as the men of Partinico could not go on strike—down tools—because they were unemployed, they would 'up tools' instead. They would hold an 'upside-down' strike—a strike in reverse. It was a delightfully simple scheme designed to call attention to the fact that Partinico was full of men only too ready and willing to go to work if given the opportunity.

On December 15th, 1955, Danilo and 60 unemployed labourers, equipped with picks and shovels, set out for the old track. They began work in the drizzling rain. They had only been working for 50 minutes when. . . .

YOU CAN'T WORK HERE !

CHARACTERS: *Danilo*
A crowd of Sicilian labourers
A Police Inspector
Carabinieri

1. Danilo and his labourers are busy filling in the holes in the track with soil and stones carried from the fields at the side of the road.

2. A Police Inspector and a party of *carabinieri* arrive. The Inspector demands that Danilo and his men stop work at once as they are breaking the law. They are trespassing with the intention of making alterations to public property. He threatens to arrest them, to order his men to charge at them with drawn batons if they do not go to their homes immediately.

3. The labourers tell him that there is no need for this; all they want is work.

4. The Inspector agrees to see about jobs for them all if they will only give up this work and return home.

5. Danilo agrees and asks his men to stop work. He leads them back to Partinico, watched by the police.

6. On the way home they complain to Danilo about giving up so easily. He tells them not to worry; the police have not heard the last of them by a long chalk. He explains that if they had carried on working, the police would have had to arrest them and it would have been their word against that of the police as to what took place. The next time he will ensure a large crowd of independent witnesses to see what takes place. They are to remember that it was the *carabinieri* who broke the law by refusing them the right to work.

To publicize his cause, Danilo travelled to Rome and appeared on Italian television. There he justified his belief in the right of all men to work and the principles underlying his 'upside down' strike.

(*Write out the text of the speech you think that Danilo would have given on television. Explain why he took 60 men on a 'strike in reverse' and what happened. End your speech by threatening to hold another 'upside down' strike on the old track of Val-guarneria if there is no work forthcoming; if the police intervene next time you and your men will not be stopped so easily.*)

In spite of their protest, conditions remained unchanged; unemployment remained a major problem. Danilo realized that he must organize another 'upside down' strike. This time, because of his television appearance, he would be able to count on a plentiful supply of photographers and press men all hungry for news.

He held a meeting in Partinico at which he outlined the object of the 'strike' for the benefit of those who were going to take part. There would be no payment for the work, and if, later on, the authorities gave their blessing to the work done and decided to employ some of the men to re-surface other roads in the area with pay, those who had been present at the 'upside down' strike were not to say: 'I worked for nothing before, therefore—I should get paid now'. If there was any work of this nature to be allocated, the most needy were to be given the first chance of it. If the police interfered again they were to sit down quietly and refuse to move, they were not to resist the police, and, as an added precaution, they were all to leave their knives at home.

A new age was about to be born, an age free from violence. Violence only breeds violence. Non-violence, as Gandhi had discovered in India, was a far more effective weapon against injustice than the flick-knife and the gun.

(*Imagine that you have decided to accompany Danilo on the second 'upside down' strike. Discuss among yourselves any questions that you would like to ask him, anything that disturbs you. Make a list of these.*

Go into your groups and show the end of the meeting. Danilo has explained his ideas and he now asks if there are any questions. Finish the scene with Danilo announcing the date of the 'strike' as the 2nd February, 1956.)

Danilo and 150 labourers set out for the second 'strike'. They made their way to the track in small groups equipped with tools for repairing the road. They were accompanied by a crowd of newsmen and photographers. Danilo's group was the first to arrive, and they began to fill in some of the pot-holes.

THE NEW AGE DAWNS

CHARACTERS: *Danilo*
              A crowd of labourers
              A Police Lieutenant
              A Police Superintendent
              A Chief Inspector
              A party of carabinieri

SCENE: On the old track of Valguarneria.

1. Danilo and his friends are filling in a pot-hole in the road.
A Police Lieutenant appears with a party of policemen.
Danilo and his friends carry on working. The Lieutenant
orders Danilo to stop work. He refuses and the Lieutenant
orders three of his policemen to escort him off the road.

2. As Danilo is walking away with the policeman he meets a
Police Superintendent hurrying to the scene. Danilo holds out
his hands to show that he is leading a peaceful demonstration,
but the Superintendent turns away.

3. Another party of police arrive armed with batons. Danilo
shouts across to them hoping that they have not come to harm
his friends.

4. The Chief Inspector of Police arrives and orders the three
policemen to release Danilo. Telling the police that he is going
back to work, he returns once more to the track where the
labourers have been waiting since his arrest. He tells them to
carry on working. The police again order him to go away.

5. The Chief Inspector, who has followed Danilo, arrives on
the scene. Danilo asks the police whether they want him to
go away or whether they mean to arrest him. The Chief
Inspector tells the men not to listen to Danilo as he is breaking

the law. The Chief Inspector and several of the police place themselves between Danilo and his friends. The men argue with the police in the background.

6. The Chief Inspector orders Danilo to send his men back to Partinico.

7. Danilo then quotes Article 4 of the Italian Constitution. 'But surely you don't believe stuff like that?' answers the Inspector. Several of the *carabinieri* laugh.

8. 'We're here to do a job', replies Danilo, 'and we're not going home until it's finished. We don't expect to be paid for it. Anyone who stops a person from working and earning his living is the same as a murderer because he is denying that man his livelihood.'

9. Several of Danilo's friends begin to chant, 'Whoever goes against us is a murderer.'

10. Hearing the word 'murderer', the police Chief becomes angry. He orders 5 *carabinieri* to arrest Danilo. Danilo immediately sits down, crosses his legs and folds his arms. The police pick him up by his feet and wrists (he is 5 feet 11 inches tall and weighs 14 stone). He offers no resistance. As he is being taken away face downwards he tells the others to carry on working and if they are arrested they are to sit down just as he has done.

Danilo was heavy and the police had to keep putting him down in the mud. At last he was placed on one of a fleet of police lorries that were standing by.

A police bugler sounded 3 blasts on a trumpet, the traditional sign for demonstrators to call off their demonstration. 'Clear off!' yelled the police.

There was no point in carrying on without their leader. They had achieved what they had set out to do: they had made a protest which had been observed by many independent witnesses. It was now time to go home. They shouldered their tools and went quietly back to Partinico.

Danilo was taken to Palermo and gaoled in the fortress prison of Ucciardone. He was joined by 4 of his friends who had been arrested among the demonstrators. They were refused bail because of 'their persistent attempts to undermine the forces of law and order'. Danilo was referred to as a 'noted political agitator'.

The trial opened at the County Court, Palermo, at 9 a.m. on the 24th March 1956.

THE TRIAL

CHARACTERS: *The Judge*
                Clerk of the Court
                Counsel for the Defence
                The Public Prosecutor
                Danilo
                Chief Inspector of Police
                The witnesses: The Rector of Florence University,
                            Carlo Levi

SCENE 1: The County Court at Palermo. Danilo stands in the dock handcuffed to a police escort. There are 2 policemen present for every 3 members of the general public.

1. The judge enters and the Clerk declares that the court is in session.
2. The Counsel for the Defence points out that the accused is handcuffed.
3. The Public Prosecutor tells the court that this was necessary 'for the maintenance of public order'.

4. The Counsel for the Defence then quotes Article 427 of the Code of Penal Procedure which states that prisoners in court should not be fettered. He asks that the accused's handcuffs be removed.

5. The Public Prosecutor has no objection to the handcuffs being taken off if the Judge is in agreement. The Judge has no objections and asks the Police Escort to remove Danilo's handcuffs.

6. The Public Prosecutor reads out the 5 charges:
   (a) Holding an illegal assembly.
   (b) Refusing to disperse when ordered to do so by the police.
   (c) Resisting arrest.
   (d) Using abusive language to a police officer.
   (e) Inciting persons to commit an offence and trespass with the intention of making alterations to public property.
   Danilo walks out of the dock and stands before the Judge's table.

7. The Judge asks Danilo to answer the charges laid against him.

8. Danilo begins by describing the death of Justina's baby. He tells the court of other injustices that he has seen. These have all been caused by poverty brought on through unemployment. He tells how the pirate trawlers have caused the fishermen to leave their homes and of his own ineffectual attempts to prohibit the pirates from fishing within the three-mile limit around the shores of western Sicily.
   He quotes Article 4 of the Italian Constitution and gives the reasons why he decided to hold an 'upside-down' strike. He explains his attempt to repair the old track, his first brush with the police, and how he called off the demonstration

because their were no witnesses. He tells of his appearance on Italian television, and of the instructions that he gave to his friends if the police stopped them from working a second time. They were to sit down quietly beside the road in protest. If allowed to carry on they were to work for 8 hours.

9. The Judge feels that if they were not going to be paid for the work, half an hour would have been long enough for them to have made their point.

10. Danilo explains that they wanted to put in a full day's work. He tells the court that they left their knives at home to avoid trouble.

11. The Judge explains that Danilo is not accused of carrying an offensive weapon.

12. The Counsel for the Defence interrupts and states that it is hinted at in the charges that Danilo and his men carried work tools to use as weapons against the police.

13. Danilo explains that by leaving their knives at home they were turning their backs upon violence.

He tells the court in detail of the events that took place when they tried to repair the road a second time. He describes why he used the term 'murderer'. He intended no offence against the police. But if he was ordered to kill someone he would refuse because it is a criminal act to take someone else's life—in the same way it is a crime to take away men's livelihood.

He tells how he was carried away by the police who had to keep putting him down in the mud because they were tired, and how he had continued to shout 'Go on working', 'Go on digging' to his friends right up to the time that he was driven away in one of the police lorries.

SCENE 2: The County Court at Palermo. 8.20 a.m. 27th March
1956.

1. The Chief Inspector of Police takes the stand. He explains
that although Danilo did not kick out at the police, he did
wave his arms about in an attempt to shake off his escort.
When Danilo was told he could go free or stay and be arrested he shouted: 'Arrest me if you can' and 'Whoever goes
against us is a murderer'. Dolci told him that according to
Article 4 of the Italian Constitution he was not breaking the
law. The Chief Inspector explains that he told Dolci that he
took his orders from Police Regulations not from the Constitution and demanded that he should return to Partinico at
once. Dolci's friends then began to insult the police shouting:
'Whoever goes against us is a murderer'. The Chief Inspector
states that he repeatedly asked Dolci to take his men home
but he refused. Dolci continued to incite the labourers who
began to argue with the police and brandish their implements
—hatchets, pickaxes, bill-hooks and spades. The fact that they
were carrying such offensive weapons proved that they did
not intend to stage a peaceful demonstration. Faced with
angry demonstrators, he had no option but to arrest Dolci
and his four friends. They all violently resisted arrest, kicking
and punching the police who were forced to immobilize
them and carry them almost bodily to the waiting lorries.

(*Many famous Italians came to the trial to speak in Danilo's
defence, friends who had known him a long time and could vouch
for his honesty of purpose. Men such as the former Rector of Florence
University, and the well-known Italian novelist Carlo Levi.*

*Imagine that you are a friend of Danilo's and you have come
to the trial to speak in his defence. Write out the speech that you
would make and use it in the trial.*)

2. The Public Prosecutor makes his closing speech. He agrees that everyone has the right to strike, but not to seek work by taking the law into his own hands. What would happen if all the unemployed decided to find work repairing things that they felt were in need of renovation? There would be chaos in a very short time. Dolci has proved his guilt by resisting arrest, and he asks the court to find the accused guilty on all 5 charges.

3. The Jury retire. (They were out for 6 hours.)

(Fade out here as in a television play or film and cut to the re-appearance of the jury back in the courtroom.)

4. The foreman of the Jury reads out the verdict. The accused is acquitted of the serious charges of 'holding an illegal assembly, refusing to disperse when ordered to do so by the police, resisting arrest and using abusive language to a police officer', but found guilty of 'inciting persons to commit an offence and trespass with the intention of making alterations to public property'.

5. The Judge sentences Danilo to 50 days imprisonment, but, as he has already been in custody for that length of time, he is free to leave the court.

6. The Prosecution angrily complains that the sentence is far too lenient.

When the trial was over, Danilo wrote his second report, *To Feed the Hungry*, which the Times Literary Supplement called a 'literary and sociological masterpiece'.

He next turned his attention to conditions in Palermo itself. By fasting again he spotlighted the plight of those living in the Cortile Cascino slums and the far worse area known as the Hole of Death. These decaying habitations were razed to the ground and the 12,000 inhabitants were moved into modern low-rental council flats.

There was still much to be done and Danilo appealed through the Italian Government for more technical assistants to help him in his work. Doctors, nurses, teachers, agronomists and social workers began to arrive, not only from Italy but from many other countries as well. Danilo Dolci Trusts were set up and members contribute financial aid to assist Danilo in his work. The British Danilo Dolci Trust sends £7000 a year to Sicily.

With financial help from abroad and with the local assistance of his technical advisers, he has created his 'Centre of Studies and Action for Full Employment' which has its headquarters in a house at the end of a cobbled street in Partinico. The Centre has 55 helpers, with other Centres at Trappeto, Roccamena, Corleone and Menfi. Here, peasants are rapidly being taught to help themselves, they are realizing that they do not have to emigrate in order to lead fuller richer lives. Each Centre has an experienced agronomist who trains the peasants in the use of the latest agricultural techniques, breaking down their ancient prejudices against the use of fertilisers and insecticides, teaching them to rotate their crops, and introducing new varieties such as hybrid maize and asparagus, so that if one crop fails they will have another crop to fall back upon rather than just give up as they used to do in the past.

Conditions are much better now than they were when Danilo first arrived on the island. The Regional Government is attempting to break up the feudal estates and apportion the land to the peasants under the Agrarian Reform Agency. The Italian Government is now pouring money into the area in order to create new industries. The peasants wages have risen to £1 a day, but there is still much to be done.

In spite of many setbacks, the dam should be in operation by 1969, and when it is completed it will irrigate a vast area down to the Gulf of Castellamare creating work for hundreds who are still unemployed. It is the only project so far that has united all the political parties. Both the Christian Democrats and the Communists are equally agreed over its benefits to the region. Danilo now wants work to begin on three more.

But the most beneficial event for the future development of Sicily has without doubt been the setting up of the Government's Anti-Mafia Commission which is attempting to rid the island of the Honoured Society. Danilo has done more than anyone to encourage the people to improve their conditions without fear of the Mafia, because he feels that so long as the Honoured Society has friends in high places there can never be any progress. He is in the forefront in this fight to the death. He has proved a courageous example of what one man can do in the face of an apparently all-powerful dictatorship. Others are now coming out of hiding to speak openly in denunciation of the Mafia's crimes. Witness after witness has appeared at the anti-Mafia trials, sometimes at great risk to themselves and their families, in order to break the age-long silence of *omerta* so that Sicily might one day be free of its greatest scourge.

Recently a Sicilian peasant summed up Danilo in the following words: 'Danilo is a serious man, he's really getting things done! Pity there are not more like him. There should be a Danilo in every village, not only in Sicily but in the whole of Italy, in every village in the world.'

THE EARTHQUAKE

In January 1968 western Sicily was struck by a series of earth tremors the combined force of which was the equivalent of the atomic bomb that fell upon Hiroshima. The villages of Montevago, Salaparuta and Gibellina were completely destroyed and the devastation spread outwards as far as Agrigento, Palermo and Trapani. In spite of the knowledge that this region lies in a notorious earthquake zone—70,000 lost their lives in Messina during the terrible earthquake of 1908—few anti-quake precautions were in operation. The frail peasant houses constructed of stone blocks ineffectively cemented together were no match for the destructive forces unleashed upon them, and they fell like ninepins trapping, maiming and killing their occupants. 300 people died in their beds during the first tremor, whereas the few houses built of reinforced concrete are still standing today. Over 500 deaths were recorded. 80,000 people left their homes to live in tent cities hastily erected by refugee organizations. Over £53,000,000 worth of damage has been done. Bands of *Mafiosi* were busy cashing in on the distress, travelling amongst the homeless offering them one tenth of the purchase price of their land and livestock with a view to making rich profits when the country eventually returns to normal.

This was but one further blow to an already stricken people. If you would like to help Danilo fight the poverty, ignorance and distress amongst the peoples of western Sicily, donations may be sent to the address given on page 85.